SOCIAL STRUCTURE AND PERSONALITY DEVELOPMENT

Social structure and personality development
The individual as a productive processor of reality

KLAUS HURRELMANN
University of Bielefeld

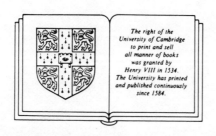

The right of the University of Cambridge to print and sell all manner of books was granted by Henry VIII in 1534. The University has printed and published continuously since 1584.

CAMBRIDGE UNIVERSITY PRESS

CAMBRIDGE

NEW YORK   NEW ROCHELLE   MELBOURNE   SYDNEY

Published by the Press Syndicate of the University of Cambridge
The Pitt Building, Trumpington Street, Cambridge CB2 1RP
32 East 57th Street, New York, NY 10022, USA
10 Stamford Road, Oakleigh, Melbourne 3166, Australia

© Cambridge University Press 1988

First published 1988

Printed in the United States of America

Library of Congress Cataloging-in-Publication Data

Hurrelman, Klaus.

Social structure and personality development: the individual as
a productive processor of reality/Klaus Hurrelmann.

p.   cm.

Bibliography: p.

Includes index.

ISBN 0-521-35474-9   ISBN 0-521-35747-0 (pbk.)

1. Socialization. 2. Social structure. 3. Personality.
I. Title.

HQ783.H87   1988

303.3′2—dc19   87–37205
                                                              CIP

British Library Cataloging-in-Publication applied for

CONTENTS

Contents

PREFACE

THIS textbook is the result of a series of lectures on sociali- zation theory that I have given at the University of Bielefeld over the last 10 years. Socialization theory is an interdisciplinary field in which the major contributions are made by sociological, psychological, and educational research. Its main concern is to investigate in what way and to what extent social, cultural, eco- nomic, and ecological structures and processes affect conditions of human personality development. Sociological research tradi- tionally focuses on asking which processes and mechanisms oper- ate within a society to assure that its members accept existing val- ues, norms, and expected behaviors. In psychological research, much attention has been paid to the question of the ways and means by which the individual develops into a competent person- ality. Educational research concentrates on the question of how the human individual and his or her social and material environ- ment can be stimulated and influenced so as to bring about a per- sonality development that meets both individual and social criteria.

The present book describes the major theoretical approaches in socialization research and summarizes the most important research findings. In this I have attempted to take into account the perspectives of all three disciplines concerned.

More recent theoretical approaches to personality development are based on the assumption that social (environmental) and psy- chological (personal) factors jointly affect the formation of per- sonality. The interactions between person and social environment are conceived as reciprocal interrelations. Approaches advocating a purely social determination of personality development are regarded as being just as obsolete as those that propose an organic and psychological maturation determined by natural laws. Instead, children, adolescents, and adults are regarded as produc- tively processing and managing external and internal reality and actively establishing and shaping relations with the societal and material environment. The concepts of education and development are applied to the entire life span and represent the lifelong process of the individual's interaction with his or her living conditions.

The chapters in this volume provide an overview of the current state of the discussion in socialization research. The first chapter introduces and explains the basic assumptions, terms, and concepts of previous socialization theory. The concepts of human development that underlie the various theories are analyzed, and it is shown how they guide the construction of theoretical concepts, the derivation of central terms, and the choice of methodological procedures. This is followed by a comparison of the sociological and psychological theories that are of major importance for socialization theory: learning theory, psychoanalysis, developmental theory, ecological psychology, systems theory, action theory, and the theory of social structure. Special attention is paid to lines of convergence between the theories that could serve as starting points for future theoretical developments.

The second chapter looks at ideas and hypotheses concerning the theoretical and methodological orientation of present-day socialization research. These ideas start from an interaction theory perspective and relate to a model of the human individual as a productive processor and manager of external and internal reality. Propositions and assumptions are sketched that could serve as a basis for a comprehensive, contextualistic concept of socialization. These ideas are taken up again in the following two chapters, where they are dealt with in more detail.

The third chapter surveys the state of research on how social and material living conditions relate to the development of individual skills and abilities. This discussion starts by investigating the research that was published in the 1960s and 1970s under the heading of "class-specific socialization in the family." After a critical appraisal of the available findings, a theoretical concept concerning the relation between social living conditions and personality development is presented, focusing on the family as the central mediator of societal reality. This is followed by an analysis of the consequences of familial socialization for school and occupational careers, and a discussion of the processes involved in adult socialization.

The fourth chapter discusses the requirements and conditions for successful and unsuccessful socialization. First, ideas on the development of action competences in childhood, adolescence, and adulthood are presented that are then drawn together to form a concept of identity. Then a review is given of the state of research on the relations between living conditions, social risk factors for stress, and psychosocial disorders of personality development. A number of strategies for intervening in the socialization process in order to prevent and overcome deviant and problem behavior are discussed. This discussion focuses on the question of what socialization research has already contributed and can yet contribute to improving the conditions for the optimal unfolding of the individual's personal competences while at the same time providing all members of society with at least a minimum of social support, solidarity, and cooperation.

For my interest in the interrelations of social structure and personality, I am largely indebted to John A. Clausen. During my studies at the University of California at Berkeley in the 1960s, he introduced me to the theoretical and empirical fundamentals of socialization research. Since then, he has repeatedly encouraged me to attempt an interdisciplinary scientific work in this field. Many of the arguments in this book are influenced by his comments and suggestions. I have also profited greatly from the work of Paul B. Baltes, Urie Bronfenbrenner, Glen H. Elder, Dieter Geulen, Jürgen Habermas, Hans Haferkamp, Barbara Heyns, Bettina Hurrelmann, Martin Kohli, Melvin L. Kohn, Richard M. Lerner, Leonard I. Pearlin, Caroline H. Persell, Rainer Silbereisen, and Dieter Ulich.

I should like to thank the students who participated in my lectures at the University of Bielefeld for the critical stimulus that led to improvements in the manuscript. I have also learned a great deal from conversations with my colleagues in the newly formed special research unit for child and adolescence research set up by the German Research Association (DFG) in Bielefeld.

I wish to thank Jonathan Harrow for his careful and sensitive translation.

Klaus Hurrelmann

Bielefeld, West Germany

1

PSYCHOLOGICAL AND SOCIOLOGICAL THEORIES OF SOCIALIZATION

THIS chapter describes the major theoretical approaches within socialization research and the basic views of human development that underlie these theories. The discussion concentrates on those chains of theory formation in psychology and sociology that have been particularly influential during the last 20 to 30 years.

AN EPISTEMOLOGICAL APPROACH

Definition of terms

The term "socialization" has been gradually gaining acceptance in scientific discussion since the beginning of the present century. The French sociologist Emile Durkheim was one of the first to introduce the term into science. He related it closely to the term "education," in that he regarded education as the most important societal means of guiding new human generations, who are "asocial" at birth, to a "social life" (Durkheim, 1968, p. 30). Today, Durkheim's use of the term appears to be sociologistic: It is mechanically geared to social adaptation and cultural assimilation and to the imprinting of human personality. More recent use of the term in the social sciences generally disregards such sociologistic components (Wentworth, 1980, p. 40). This has led to a situation in which the term socialization has increasingly caught the interest of the scientific disciplines of psychology and education, where it has found wide acceptance in recent years.

1

Social structure and personality development

To avoid any misunderstanding, let me begin by offering my own definitions of socialization, personality development, and education.

Socialization. Socialization in my view, is the process of the emergence, formation, and development of the human personality in dependence on and in interaction with the human organism, on the one hand, and the social and ecological living conditions that exist at a given time within the historical development of a society on the other. Socialization designates the process in the course of which a human being, with his or her specific biological and psychological disposition, becomes a socially competent person, endowed with the abilities and capacities for effective action within the larger society and the various segments of society, and dynamically maintains this status throughout the course of his or her life.

Personality development. The term "personality" is applied as part of the definition of socialization. Personality designates a person's particular organized structure of motives, attributes, traits, attitudes, and action competences that is the biographical product of coping with environmental and organismic demands. Personality development can be described as the sequential long-term changes in essential elements of this structure in the course of time and during the course of life.

Education. The term "education" must be clearly distinguished from the term "socialization." Education is a logical subconcept of the concept of socialization that designates the actions and activities by which persons attempt to influence the personality development of others in order to advance them according to specific values. The term education covers only a part of the socially conveyed influences on personality development that are grouped under the term socialization, namely, the conscious and planned exertions of influence in the sense of social interventions.

This definition of terms provides the primary focus for the argument of this book. The definitions have intentionally been left flexible, so that different theories can be related to them. The definition of socialization given here does not restrict scientific analysis of the area of research to a fixed theoretical and methodological position but leaves enough room for the largest possible number of interpretations.

Psychological and sociological theories

Basic theoretical assumptions

Theories that use the concept of socialization accept two basic elementary assumptions that are essential to socialization theory.

The first basic assumption is that *socially conveyed influences on the development of personality actually exist.* The term socialization implicitly suggests the development of personality and the process of social interaction and social change and, through this conceptual link, already asserts that social factors influence human development. The term socialization conveys the idea that no dimensions of the human personality are formed without societal influence but that they are continually realized in a concrete living situation that affects the unfolding of the features of personality.

The second basic assumption is that *a human being can become a subject who is capable of social action only through assimilation into and active dealing with the social and material environment.* Only through this process can the various features and traits of a personality take shape and be modified and reshaped from one phase of life to the next; only in this way will a person be able to come to terms with his or her environment, behave in accordance with the demands of this environment, and, at the same time, have an influence on the formation of that environment.

The way in which these conceptually implicit assumptions about socialization are individually formulated and transformed into specific statements differs according to the theoretical approach taken. It is natural that sociological theories place more emphasis on the social conditions of personality development, whereas psychological theories place much greater emphasis on organismic and mental factors. All effective theories of socialization, however, must allow for the "double nature" of personality development that is both societal and individual and, for this reason, cannot build on one-sided theoretical premises (cf. Goslin, 1969, p. 17; Clausen, 1986b, p. 22).

Recent years have seen a growing similarity and a bridging between the different premises taken by sociology and psychology. The contributions of authors from different disciplines that are brought together in the handbook of socialization research by Hurrelmann and Ulich (1982) and the articles and books by Lerner (1975), Kohli (1980), Elder (1979, 1985), Baltes and Brim (1979), Wentworth (1980), Kerckhoff and Corwin (1981),

3

Oerter and Montada (1987), Dollase (1985), and Clausen (1986a) have already indicated common views on many points and in many dimensions.

In this volume I will attempt to integrate a number of different positions and perspectives in the area of personality development, starting from an initial position in the social sciences. As a first step in this venture, it is necessary to investigate the epistemological foundations of theory formation in this field. The design and construction of a theory can be understood only if the more general basic assumptions that underlie the processes of theory formation are also taken into account. In the following discussion, a "theory" is understood as an interrelated and internally conclusive structure of assumptions and statements about an area of research (in this case, personality development).

Epistemological assumptions and theory formation

Epistemological orientations and assumptions are present in all areas of scientific work, and thus also in socialization research. These orientations and assumptions are metatheoretical and metamethodological modelings of the object of investigation. Most theories of personality development and socialization are based on a particular model projection of the individual and/or the society. Proceeding from this model, the theories define the object of investigation and make fundamental statements about its nature. This procedure determines the methods and goals of scientific analysis, because it sets the criteria for the choice of central terms and concepts and their application and interconnection, the criteria for the choice of methodological procedures and their application, and also the criteria for determining the central thematic content for the development of theory and methodology.

The concept of socialization is a scientific construct that describes a portion of reality that is not directly observable for descriptive and analytic purposes. Socialization is an object of investigation that exists in reality but cannot be materially grasped. A model that serves as a focal point for epistemological orientations and assumptions helps to make this complex area of investigation conceptually accessible.

The model chosen is often a metaphor drawn from either the scientific or the everyday world. Thus, for example, metaphors of the person as a physical machine or as a biological organism are found particularly in psychological research. Metaphors of the person as calculating maximizer of utility or player of social roles are found particularly in sociological research into personality development. Any model makes a considerable simplification and selection of aspects of reality, and in this way reduces the complexity of the object of investigation. It presents a more or less arbitrary and plausible arrangement by the scientist, but its claims to validity do not permit further derivation or justification by argument. The one and only thing that counts is the heuristic efficiency of the model in the process of theory formation and methodologically guided research (Wagner, 1984).

In the sociological and psychological theories of personality development, several different models of the person have always existed side by side as a focal point for epistemological orientations and assumptions. Often one of the models, with its respective theoretical and methodological variants, has predominated during a particular historical phase, but other models always remain in the background that may become central in a later historical phase (Looft, 1973; Geulen, 1977). It is probable that such a plurality of epistemological orientations and assumptions, with their respective theoretical and methodological variants, will remain a feature of the theory of personality development.

In the last 10 to 20 years, however, two processes stand out that indicate that some fundamental changes have been occurring in the formation of socialization theory. First of all, in recent years the need to make explicit the epistemological orientations and assumptions that underlie their theory formation and their methodological and empirical strategies appears to have become increasingly self-evident to every group of scientists. This, in turn, has led to better comprehension of the fundamental positions and the principles of construction applied in the theory and methods used by other groups of scientists, and thus makes them reconstructable and criticizable. Greater awareness of epistemological orientations and assumptions makes it possible to assess both theoretical and methodological procedures in the context of the general structure of an epistemological strategy. This makes it easier to identify the relations between concrete individual theories and methodological procedures. An increased awareness of the way in which the choice of theory and method depends on the model should, in the long run, increase the willingness of scientific groups to cooperate in those areas of research in which the meta-theoretical and metamethodological starting points are not too divergent or even indicate points of agreement.

Second, in recent years there has been a noticeable closing of the gap between the epistemological orientations and assumptions in psychological and sociological research into personality development. Scientific groups are increasingly moving away from the stereotyped views of human beings that predominated in the past and are turning to more complex and differentiated models as focal points for epistemological assumptions. The extremely simple, metaphorlike views of human beings are gradually being outgrown, especially those that placed a one-sided emphasis on either the organic or social determinants of human development. In their place, more differentiated models are being developed that see the relation between the person and the environment, between individual and society, as the heart of their concern (cf. Featherman and Lerner, 1985; Hurrelmann, 1985; Overtone and Reese, 1973).

If we attempt to seek out the essential model projections at this more differentiated and more complex stage, we arrive at the four models of the relation between person and environment that are briefly presented in the next section. I shall not attempt to describe each model in detail; my object is simply to outline briefly, in a shorthand, idealized form, models of the relation between person and environment that have prevailed within psychology and sociology during the last three decades.

Basic models of the relation between person and environment

The mechanistic model. This model assumes the environment as given and as the cause of a person's behavior. Developmental impulses come from outside the organism. As a result, changes in behavior are interpreted as consequences, as responses to specific environmental conditions. An individual's development is understood as a result of the sum of these responses or also an as adaptation to the norms and values that are defined by the environment. Development is conceived as a permanent change in the person's feature and traits. It has no inherent end or goal and is never completed, since the individual adopts the demands and expectations that are fed by the environment into his or her personality structure until the end of life.

The organismic model. In this model, the impulses for human development are assumed to lie within the organism. Development is a process of natural growth that proceeds according to specific, recognizable laws or rules that possess general validity. It is considered to be typical for human development that the individual develops some organizational schemes for the processing of the information and impulses offered by the environment. The process of development follows specific qualitative sequences and sequentially ranked stages that develop out of the preceding stages, and the environment has either a stimulating or a restricting effect on the speed of development. The development is aimed toward a goal or end inherent in the organism, namely the achievement of the qualitatively highest stage of development.

The systemic model. In this model the impulses for human development are assumed to result from the reciprocal adaptation and interpenetration of person and environment as psychological or social systems. In the process of development, a person absorbs, step-by-step, the expectations and behavioral rules of the social system, until they become internalized and self-effective motivational forces and goals for the person's own action. Social and psychological systems interpenetrate one another and, in the course of their development, level off at certain more or less stable states of balance. Thus there is no fixed goal or end of human development, though the reciprocal relation between person and environment strives toward a state of balance. The optimal unfolding of personal needs and actions is possible only in this state.

The contextualistic model. In this model, human development is seen as a lifelong process of interaction between the social and material environment and the human organism. The individual finds him- or herself in a permanent process of acquisition from and confrontation with the social environment. Although the individual's behavior is shaped by his or her successive contexts, the individual actively seeks some situations and rejects others, within the limits of social and individual constraints. He or she chooses specific means to attain specific goals, considers the consequences of the corresponding action, and takes into account that these consequences change the contextual conditions for his or her own actions. This model contains no inherent goal or end point for human development. However, the acquisition of social and cultural action competences that help a person to act autonomously in the social environment and to form his or her own identity is seen as the criterion for successful development.

The four epistemological models for the formation of theory and the choice of method in research into socialization processes should not be seen as completely homogeneous in themselves and totally separated from each other. There are several points of contact that offer possibilities for syntheses. Nevertheless, each of the models can serve as a starting point for individual theoretical and methodological concepts. According to the main theoretical traditions of both sociology and psychology, learning theory positions conform most closely to the mechanistic model; psychoanalytic and the cognitive developmental theory positions to the organismic model; ecological and systems theory positions to the systemic model; and action theory and the theory of social structure to the contextualistic model. A closer analysis of some of the most important theories from traditional psychology and sociology, given in the following section, at the same time reveals that even when clear reference is made to one epistemological model, many points of agreement between the different theories can be found.

Which of these models the individual scientist selects as the basis and starting point for the formation of theories and the choice of method finally depends on factors in the scientific process that are hard to evaluate. Such factors, for example, include educational background, level of experience, and also the personal history of the individual scientist. The process of converting the metatheoretical and metamethodological model into theoretical and methodological constructions is also hard to analyze, because it does not follow any generally accepted criteria that are shared by the scientific community but depends instead on conventions that have undergone changes during the course of the development of science – conventions that determine what is acceptable as a suitable conversion of a model projection into theory and methods. As a rule, in a first step metatheoretical models are replaced by very general theories that contain a series of "empty spaces" which, in turn, have to be filled by specific and direct object-related theories (Eckensberger, 1979).

In the next two sections of this chapter, I will explore some fundamental theoretical approaches to the analysis of the relations between person and environment, in order to evaluate their usefulness for socialization theory. Both psychological and sociological theories will be examined to see how they explain the genesis and development of the human personality as a product of interaction with social and material living conditions. This analysis should produce suggestions for the development of a comprehensive concept of socialization.

PSYCHOLOGICAL THEORIES: SOCIAL LEARNING THEORY, PSYCHOANALYSIS, DEVELOPMENTAL THEORY, AND ECOLOGICAL THEORY

In psychology, it is, above all, concepts from social learning theory, psychoanalysis, cognitive developmental theory, and ecological theory that have proved important for the analysis of human developmental processes in interaction with the social and material environment. Each of these approaches will be dealt with briefly here. Their basic positions will be sketched, and their importance for the analysis and explanation of socialization will be discussed.

Social learning theory

Classical learning theory approaches employ the mechanistic model of the relations between person and environment. The goal is to explain human behavior as a result of the responses to impulses from the environment. Human behavior is not regarded as being influenced either by genetic factors or by the effect of maturation processes. Rather, it is attributed to the processing of experiences with environmental influences. In this respect, learning theory has, from its very beginnings, been opposed to the concept of development as a fixed sequence of qualitative steps of features or competences of a person that develop out of each other, a view found in some developmental theories in psychology.

Conceptual foundations

Learning theory assumes that human beings enter the world without innately established behavioral schemes and must first construct their behavior with the help of experiences and their processing of them. Forms of behavior and action competences are formed only through such learning processes. Accordingly, the goal of learning theory is to explain the mechanisms and their regularities by which ways of behaving are built up through different forms and structures of learning processes. One of the main mechanisms of learning is considered to be reinforcement. The occurrence of reinforcement determines whether a response, once learned, will be produced or reproduced. In modern social learning theory, the effects of reinforcement are no longer seen as automatic, as was assumed in some classical approaches. The effect of reinforcement depends on how the relationship between an act and its consequence is perceived by the subject and how the probabilities of consequences are assessed. Thus, in the more recent versions of learning theory, cognitive processes are incorporated to a greater degree than in the early versions (Maccoby and Martin, 1984, p. 5).

Recent learning theory approaches pay much attention to the regulation of learning by social influences and relationships. In Albert Bandura's (1977, 1986) theory, which was most influential in this field, each person processes that which he or she perceives about persons in their functions as "social models." This is done in such a way that the person acquires an implicit construction of rule systems from the behavior of others through perception, attribution of meaning, cognitive structuring, information selection, information weighting, and so forth. Accordingly, children and adults construct conceptual schemes and generative rule systems that effectively guide their behavior through active dealing or contact with other people and an active style of information processing. Learning through social models occurs predominantly through the observer's identification with and imitation of a behavior presented by another person (Bandura, 1977, p. 105). The model need not be physically present for the model's behav-

Psychological and sociological theories

ior to be acquired; under certain circumstances, the cognitive representation of others' behavior will have the same effects.

Although this theory is geared to isolated relations between, as a rule, two persons and disregards more complex structures of human interaction, we have here a theoretical version of learning theory that is of value for the further development of socialization theory, and from which one can anticipate important contributions for the explanation of socialization processes. Its special value is that it postulates, as a central component of the concept of learning theory, the permanent lifelong ability of the individual to learn. This concept makes it possible to explain lasting changes in personality features that affect the new acquisition, as well as the unlearning or forgetting, of behavioral tendencies as related to an increasing differentiation of behavior and an increasing generalization of responses to similar situations. In this modern learning theory, change through learning includes different functional areas of personality, such as cognitive structure, motives, attitudes, evaluations, and self-regulation.

Thus, modern learning theory gives prominence to the postulate of autonomous human activity. Recent approaches distance themselves from the mechanical concept of stimulus–response connections predominant in classical learning theory approaches (Skinner, 1938) and stress the importance of the processing and structuring of experiences in a process that each individual steers according to his or her own principles. The individual's own activity, creativity, and self-efficacy are given much weight in this approach. Learning is no longer considered to be a passive reception but an active acquisition, processing, and structuring of experiences (Ulich, 1980, p. 91).

Critical assessment

In the search for the mechanisms for the building of complex construction and regulation systems, the modern approaches of learning theory pay much attention not only to the mechanisms but also to the content of the learning process and stress the construction of behavioral and action competences as an integral part of the process of active interaction with the social and material environment. In recent years theories of learning have also attempted, along with the short-term, to consider the more long-term and

11

stable changes in individual information processing, and the subsequent construction of regulatory systems, that lead to competent behavior. These theories have made important contributions to the analysis of environmental influences on personality development. Since the newer approaches also attempt to relate the sequence of developmental stages to specific starting constellations in the person–environment relation, learning theories are also of increasing importance for the theory of personality development. Thus, modern learning theory offers concepts that are of direct significance for the analysis of socialization processes.

Psychoanalysis

Psychoanalytic theories of human development are based on the organismic model of the relations between person and environment, according to which the decisive impulses for the unfolding of a personality are powers that are found within the organism.

Conceptual foundations

Sigmund Freud, the most important founder of psychoanalysis, did not conceive his theory as a theory of socialization but as a theory oriented toward clinical psychology. He himself paid relatively little attention to children and adolescents and, in his research and clinical practice, worked almost exclusively with adults. Nevertheless, the concept of personality development that underlies his work is, without doubt, very important for socialization theory. His observation that the neurotic illnesses of his adult patients had their origins in early childhood had important consequences for our understanding of the developmental history of the normal child. Freud used the reconstruction of the childhood experiences of emotionally disturbed adults to throw light on the course of the psychosexual development of his patients and basically pointed to the interaction processes that occur between parents, children, and other reference persons in the course of which the psychological structures develop. In this sense, Freud's concept contains a hidden analysis of the relationship between person and social environment that he himself did not work out in sufficient detail.

Psychological and sociological theories

Freud provides a structural analysis of the personality that stresses the relationship of tension between internal motives and drives and the social culture with its norms and sanctions and thus touches upon important analytic aspects of the process of socialization (see Freud, 1949). As Busch (1985, p. 31) worked out, in his analysis of the socialization dimensions of Freud's theory, social psychological chains of argumentation appear in Freud's work after his discovery of the mental events of identification, narcissism, and superego. Identification is revealed as a mode in which the individual masters the social and material world of "objects." Freud sees the process of identification with a loved one as a preliminary stage of object choice and traces it back to autoerotic and narcissistic forms of "incorporation." Identification is also related to imitation and empathy and opens access to the mental life of another person. By conceiving identification as an alignment with another ego that is imitated and emotionally grasped, Freud provided a concept for the process of internalization that is also of interest to sociology (Freud, 1923).

Psychoanalytic theory is essentially the attempt to explain the origins and the construction of the personality as resulting from the direct sensory relation of a person to emotionally important other persons. In this relation, the sympathetic attention and orientation toward another person is regarded as an essential impulse of human development. This potential of psychoanalytic theory has, however, not been conceptually developed, because of the strong emphasis on drive theory (represented by the powerful psychological figure of the id, the unconscious part of the personality structure consisting of instinctual, aggressive, and sexual impulses). The tension between the id and the superego (the part of the personality structure which has internalized the values and rules of the society) that is held in balance by the control authority of the ego is thereby reduced, in many of Freud's works, to a type of anthropological natural constant. His vision, which was so sharp when he analyzed individuals, clouded over as soon as he tried to trace the sociocultural conditions of personality beyond the range of the family, despite his consideration of sensuality, on the one hand, and social norm systems on the other (Busch, 1985, p. 38).

Social structure and personality development

Critical assessment

If Freud's approach is to be used in socialization theory, it must be freed from its fixation on drive theory and released from its somewhat excessive concentration on the human organism. It then promises the discovery that sensory aspects function as a basis of social experience and as an unconscious background for apparently rational and intentional actions. At the same time it allows an analysis of the influence of social actualities on the formation of the relationships between child and parent and the mastering of relationship crises during personality development.

E. H. Erikson was a decisive pioneer in the transformation of psychoanalytic concepts that are relevant for socialization theory. He campaigned for the inclusion of elements of drive theory in a social psychological frame of personality theory. He worked on the social and cultural-historical influences on the structure of the family and thus opened up psychoanalytic theory to elements of sociological theory. The concrete composition of the social environment thus became part of his theory of personality development. Moreover, he no longer excluded the conscious processes that a person applies to coordinate the sensory basis with the behavioral demands of the social environment. Personality development, also understood as life history, is reflected in this theory in the interdependent processes of the organization of the human body, the organizing of experience through ego synthesis, and the social organization of individuals in society (Erikson, 1959, p. 52). Thus he introduced three units of analysis that can be found in many present-day socialization theories.

Some more recent variants of psychoanalytic theory have extended Erikson's approach and elaborate the emergence of a sensory structure in the physical interchange with the mother and other persons with whom the child has an intimate relationship. The construction of the child's inner personal structure is conceived as being initially an unconscious construction of forms of interaction mirroring the familial practice, which is itself influenced by societal conditions. This finally overcomes Freud's socially blind drive concept and develops a differentiated socialization concept in which the tension between sensuality and social norms becomes the focus of analysis (cf. Lorenzer, 1972). These modern psychoanalytic approaches are of great significance for overcoming the disciplinary boundaries within the theory of personality development.

Cognitive developmental theory

In contrast to the psychoanalytic theory of personality development, another very influential theory also refers to the organismic model, namely, Piaget's cognitive developmental theory. In his theory Piaget concentrated particularly on developmental processes in youth and adolescence.

Conceptual foundations

Personality development is understood as a systematic process of the construction of abilities, deeply rooted in biological dimensions, that, step-by-step, enables a person to make a flexible and actively steered adjustment to environmental conditions. Piaget endeavors to work out the regulatory cognitive schemes for the process of acquiring and processing the information and impulses that are presented to persons by the environment. According to him, these schemes can be categorized in specific qualitative developmental stages that have a sequential order (Piaget, 1970).

The focus of Piaget's epistemological interest lies in the explanation of the development of human intelligence, but his approach can also be applied to other dimensions of personality development. He regards "intelligence" as a broad categorical term for the potential of human behavior coordination and its reflection. The human capacity for knowledge, its structure, and its efficiency should be explained through the reciprocal processes of exchange between the organism and the environment. "Adaptation" serves as a basic function of the organism, in the sense of a necessary and continuously reapplied adjustment to the environment by each human organism at every stage of development. This adaptation is also always a process of actively shaping the environment, with the goal that subsequent exchange processes between organism and environment should favorably serve the further development of the organism.

The biologically oriented basic model for this theory includes the idea of development through self-regulatory behavior. The development of intelligence is influenced by several factors, such as inheritance, maturation, the experience of effects on objects ("material experience"), and social communication and education ("social experience"). In this process, the factor "equilibration" coordinates the influences of predisposition and material and social experience, and shapes them into a structured framework (Piaget, 1950).

The human organism is conceived by Piaget as a self-regulating system in which structures are present to the extent that they express momentary states of balance in the exchange between organism and environment. These relatively stable states gradually turn into persisting features that Piaget labels "stages of development." For the cognitive development of personality, he differentiates between the state of sensorimotor intelligence (0 to 18 months of life); the preoperational stage (18 months to 7 years); the stage of concrete operations (7 to 12 years); and the stage of formal operations (12 years and older). The aim of his analysis is to attempt to identify the mechanisms by which individuals develop knowledge, in the sense of rational problem solving and potential scientific thinking.

Piaget's developmental theory stresses the active adjustment of the organism as it confronts the environment. For Piaget, cognitive development is a spontaneous process that the child sets in motion independently and maintains through active interaction with the social and material environment. In contrast to learning theory, Piaget stresses the regularities and laws in the construction of mechanisms and regulatory schemes of the person's interaction with the environment. In this respect, his theory is most relevant for socialization theory.

Beginning with a biological-organismic orientation, Piaget develops the concept of a human organism that is characterized by spontaneous and constructive activity. He discards simple reductionist models and works on a differentiated concept of constructive and active relations of exchange and interaction between person and environment. His theoretical statements relate to a lifelong process of development and are not restricted to single sections of the life history.

Critical assessment

Whereas the strength of developmental theory lies in its firm theoretical reconstruction of the active process of exchange between person and environment, the concept of the environment itself is, in comparison, less differentiated and oddly passive. This weakness is linked to the biological roots of organismic thinking and the concept of adaptation. For the organismic concept of this design, it is of little interest which concrete form the social and material environments take. The environment is understood only as a sort of medium for personality development, whereas its direct properties are of lesser significance. As Herzog (1984, p. 194) points out, Piaget maps out a theoretical design in which development needs something to work on; what this "something" specifically is does not matter. What the individual is acting upon is unimportant. The object of action is secondary; only the action itself is important. The only necessity is that some object must be present. The environment is significant only insofar as it provides opportunities for action.

Although Piaget talks about an exchange between the human organism and the environment, a balanced relationship is not implied. Human behavior and action are a function of the organism, and the environment influences the organism only to the extent that it has to be incorporated into the existing structures of the organism. The environment has no intrinsic determining significance for the organism, since the organism, to a certain extent, constructs its epistemological instruments in a self-referential manner. What Piaget does not stress sufficiently is that the person lives in an environment that is not only biologically suitable but also, to a large extent, constructed by human beings and bears the mark of human action and work.

Without doubt, the contribution of Piaget's approach has been to work out fundamental laws of the human developmental process that also take account of the possibilities and limits of external influences. However, he has not paid enough attention to the importance of concrete forms of social interaction within social groups and the significance of the concrete shaping of material and social living conditions for the development of personality. As Seiler (1980, p. 115) has pointed out, Piaget has underestimated the importance of social factors. Moreover, it appears that he assumes that the intrinsic equilibration process of the structures inevitably leads to adapted systems. Although one can grant him that social necessities are partially reflected in these equilibration processes, he does not show this clearly enough, and in the concrete reconstruction of these structures he does not give this enough weight.

In more recent versions of cognitive developmental theory, it can clearly be seen that more attention has been paid to social environmental components, in order to reduce the deficits in Piaget's approach. It is increasingly accepted that accelerations or delays during the course of the developmental stages of cognitive competences are dependent on the level of stimulation in the social and material environment and that this stimulation, in turn, relates to the structure and the quality of the social interaction between a developing person and the people with whom he or she closely relates. Corresponding research into cognitive and moral development shows that in certain sociocultural constellations the highest stages of development either are not reached or are reached only after a long delay (Kohlberg, 1963; Doise and Palmonari, 1984). This is just a short distance from theoretical acceptance of the significance of the sociostructural and socioecological nature of the environment.

Developmental theory, in this expanded version, contributes greatly to explaining the role that social factors play in the construction of an individual's cognitive and social competences. It can particularly help answer the question of which conditions affect the stimulus potential of the social and material environment in such a way that a more or less supportive development of individual competences results. Interesting research approaches and theoretical concepts that take up these aspects have become increasingly prominent in recent research (Edelstein and Habermas, 1984).

Ecological theory

Ecological theory also starts from the organismic model of the relations between person and environment, though it has, in addition, many points of agreement with the systemic model. The proponents of this approach are concerned with analyzing the effects of the concrete nature of the human living space on personality development. Thus, this position approaches the more sociologically oriented socialization theories, which is also expressed, for example, in the criticism aimed at maturation theory and all one-sided organism-related developmental theories in psychology.

Conceptual foundations

At present the leading proponent of ecological theory is Urie Bronfenbrenner. In his theory, the ecology of human development is concerned with the progressive reciprocal accommodation between the developing person and the changing properties of his or her living space. This process is continually influenced by the interrelations between the immediate living space and the larger contexts of social structure in which it is embedded (Bronfenbrenner, 1979).

Bronfenbrenner adopts from Piaget the concept of the active individual who creatively adapts to his or her environment but goes farther than Piaget, in that he additionally assumes an active environment. For Bronfenbrenner, the developing person is a growing, dynamic unit who progressively takes command of and reshapes the world in which he or she lives. Since the environment also exerts influences, and thus a process of mutual adaptation is both possible and necessary, the relation between person and environment is understood as being truly a reciprocal one (Bronfenbrenner, 1977, 1978).

Bronfenbrenner develops a theoretical system that not only analyzes a person's immediate living areas (i.e., microsystems of actions, social relationships, and roles within actual local space) but also covers living conditions and environmental events that lie outside it. With progressive development, a person gains access to living areas outside the microsystem and develops the ability to link together the different influences of various living areas. Bronfenbrenner regards human development as a permanent change in the ways in which individuals grasp and confront the environment. He sees human development as the process through which the developing person acquires expanded, more differentiated, and more reliable ideas about his or her environment. Through this, a person becomes motivated toward and equipped for activities and actions that enable him or her to recognize the properties of the environment, or even to recognize and reshape it (Bronfenbrenner, 1979, chapter 3).

Bronfenbrenner's conceptual framework can be used to analyze the developmentally supportive potential of a living area. Living areas are classified as encouraging development to the extent that they enable the developing person to participate in increasingly more complex actions (understood as complex action sequences with a specific goal structure), interpersonal relationships, and social role structures. The state of an individual's development is revealed by the degree of intrinsic variety and structural complexity of the actions in which he or she is involved. This state of development also depends on stimulation from other people as these become a part of a person's environment.

Critical assessment

It is clear that Bronfenbrenner's approach overcomes the limitations of organismic thinking found in the psychological theories. He presents a context-related theory of personality development that is supported by concrete empirical findings from psychological research. Bronfenbrenner works with a model of the relations between person and environment that combines elements of the organismic model with a systems model. It is reminiscent, on the one hand, of Piaget's concept of active adjustment to the environment, and, on the other, of the concept of balance between person and environment that is accepted by modern systems theorists. By placing the concept of "activity" in a central position, Bronfenbrenner also refers to concepts from the materialist psychology of personality.

In contrast to both psychoanalytic approaches and Piaget's theory, Bronfenbrenner's theory has no concept of a fixed sequence of stages of intellectual or moral development. A certain orientation toward learning theory is noticeable here, in which development is understood as the respective sum of stimulating impulses from the social environment. For Bronfenbrenner, the development of the personality does not follow any set sequence of phases that need to build on one another, and it is not aimed at some goal or end point but can, in principle, be infinitely shaped and influenced. However, each step of the transfer from one living area to another, and each extension of a person's radius of social action, requires an extension of the relevant specific abilities and competences.

As this discussion has shown, in the ecological approach to developmental psychology environmental influences are recognized as important conditions for human personality development and are given a central position in theory formation. The interactive embedding of the formation of cognitive and social structures by children, adolescents, and adults, which, for many years was postulated only by sociological socialization research, is expressly taken into account. Features of interaction processes are regarded as conditions for the construction of individual competences, and the extent to which they encourage the development of personality is investigated (cf. Silbereisen and Eyferth, 1986).

A critical point is the fact that the concrete investigations that have been carried out in the tradition of ecological developmental theory are restricted to the level of microanalytic studies and neglect the relations among different features of the interaction situation and more comprehensive conditions of social structure. The question of how the microstructure of living conditions is related to the macrostructure, the organization of economical, political, and social actualities, is only peripherally addressed. Nevertheless, the model of the embedding of the immediate living space in concentrically arranged living areas that reciprocally influence one another should prove very fruitful for further theory building. Moreover, it provides a clear presentation of the processes by which material and social living conditions are transformed into psychological structures.

Conclusion

This examination of four psychological theories of personality development clearly shows – despite all the differences – how strong are the points of agreement among the different approaches. All of the recent variants share the assumption that the development of personality can be understood and explained only by the relationship between the individual and his or her environment. Social learning theory and ecological approaches place great value on the analysis of the concrete composition of the person's environment and thus show specific similarities to the sociological theories that will be presented in the following section of this chapter.

Additionally, the convergence between psychological and sociological theories is expressed by the fact that in recent psychological theory there has been a growing orientation toward the systemic and contextualistic models that are the basis of several sociological theories. For example, Lerner and Busch-Rossnagel (1981) have developed a concept of "dynamic interactionism" that includes the interactive relations between individual and environment within a systems theory framework. They thereby conceive a probability theory version of developmental sequences in the individual life history in which biological factors (genetic endowment and physical features), psychological factors (temperament and cognitive style), and societal factors (social living conditions and historical events) are understood as equally important factors of personality development that exist in a state of mutual dynamic dependence. Similar attempts to combine learning theory, ecological theory, systems theory, and interaction theory can be found in the work of Riegel (1975) and Magnusson and Allen (1983).

These ideas have been taken up and more fully developed by Featherman and Lerner (1985), who call their theoretical perspective "developmental contextualism." They suggest that the study of human development should be placed within the context of commonalities and variations of behavioral change over the life span that characterize cohorts, sociocultural classes, sexes, and other subpopulations of a given society at a particular historical moment. The lifelong potential for psychological and behavioral development among human beings is seen as an evolved biosocial phenomenon. The authors propose a methodology for distinguishing the features of development from change in general by using the concept of time-dependent frequences and rates of succession of events – that is, changes whose probabilities of occurring are linked to prior events or states, in a probabilistic relationship (Featherman and Lerner, 1985, p. 660).

In life-span developmental psychology, the importance of historical and sociocultural influences on individual development are recognized. Along with the factors that are traditionally taken into account in developmental psychology, societal and biographical variables thus are also acknowledged. For example, in analyzing the development of intraindividual and interindividual changes in human personality, Baltes, Reese, and Lipsitt (1980, p. 75) differentiate among developmental conditions that relate to age, cultural change, and life events. Developmental conditions that are linked to the age of a person are, for example, age-specific social expectations, tasks, and rights that are uniformly directed at all members of an age group. Developmental conditions that relate to cultural change are those that are produced by historical events and that affect all members of a generation – for example, economic crises and technological innovations. Developmental conditions that relate to life events are important for individual life histories and thus affect individuals according to random criteria but do not affect age or generation groups as a whole. Examples are the death of a parent, serious illnesses, divorce, and other so-called critical life events that produce an abrupt change in the living situation (Dohrenwend and Dohrenwend, 1974).

All of the psychological approaches presented here share a concept of development in which changes in individual features, attitudes, and action competences are produced on the basis of the particular previous experiences that result from confrontation with physical and organic developments, on the one hand, and environmental actualities on the other. It is here that one finds the most important points of agreement with sociological theory.

SOCIOLOGICAL THEORIES: SYSTEMS THEORY, ACTION THEORY, AND THE THEORY OF SOCIAL STRUCTURE

In sociology, ideas from systems theory, action theory, and the theory of social structure have, in the last two decades, proved to be particularly significant for the analysis of the process of the individual's interaction with his or her environment. In this section I shall briefly describe these three theoretical traditions and explore their importance for socialization theory.

Systems theory

Sociological systems theory has its roots in the functionalist theory that is oriented toward the organismic model of the relations between person and environment. In this early version, society is understood in terms of an analogy to biological organisms. The

Social structure and personality development

American sociologist Talcott Parsons adopted this way of thinking and transformed it into a sociological theory. The concept of functionality retains a central position in Parson's theory as it describes the effect of a social element that contributes to the realization of a specific state of balance and integration of a social system.

Conceptual foundations

Parsons's functionalist systems theory developed a systematic sociological conception of the relations between individual and society. He made a particular effort to synthesize the microperspective of individual psychological dynamics and the macroperspective of societal social structures. The main analytic tool that he used was the concept of functionally related and specifically structured constellations and features that he called "systems." In his analysis, he differentiated between an *organic system,* a *psychological system,* and a *social system* (Parsons, 1964).

The organic system of human personality forms the basis of all human action. It supplies the personality with the necessary energy for basic physiological and psychological functions. The main task of the psychological system of personality is to control these drive energies and to direct them in socially acceptable and prescribed channels. Personality is essentially characterized by this structure of need dispositions that develop into stable features during the course of the internalization of societal controls. In this part of his approach, Parsons closely followed psychodynamic theories, in particular Freud's psychoanalysis, from which he also derived his assumptions about developmental theory (Parsons, 1964, p. 93).

Parsons separated the organic system from the social and the personality system. The social system is formed from the patterns of relationships among different actors in their positions as representatives of specific social roles. A social role is defined through the normative expectations that are directed at the actor by members of social reference groups and institutions. In Parsons's theory, socialization is the process of assimilating and internalizing the values and role norms of the social environment (Parsons and Bales, 1955).

During the process of socialization, the actor absorbs, step-by-step, the expectations and behavioral standards of the social system until they become internalized goals and self-effective motivational forces for his or her own action and form the personality system. The child thus acquires the cultural patterns of meaning that are necessary to initially constitute his or her personality system. Personality system and social system are thus essentially made up of the same components. The process of socialization is completed with the internalization of the most comprehensive of the surrounding social systems, namely the system of the society. The process is made up by acquiring normative and social structures step-by-step during the course of life (Parsons and Bales, 1955).

In Parsons's theory, the precondition for the realization of human action is the "agreement" among the three systems of organism, personality, and society. These systems interpenetrate, and during the course of their development they level off at certain more or less stable states of balance. In Parsons's concept, the idea of balance is postulated as the goal state of each single system in its relation to each other system. In this sense, through the process of socialization, an agreement is reached between the needs of the organism, the personality, and the social structure of society.

For Parsons, an individual's history of socialization consists of running through a hierarchy of variously structured and increasingly more differentiated role relationships. From the relationship between mother and child during the preoedipal phase, across the role system of the small nuclear family, Parsons draws extended lines of role relationships in peer groups and school that become more complicated during the phase of adolescence, until the complex role fields of adults in profession, family, and society are reached (Parsons, 1964, p. 161). Each person moves through increasingly more complex role structures and must interact with the reciprocal expectations in the various role relationships that alter in the different phases of the individual life history. This process is more or less completed with the internalization of behavioral expectations and value orientations and their fixing in the structure of individual need dispositions.

Social structure and personality development

Critical assessment

Parsons delivered a comprehensive and differentiated theory that overcame many of the shortcomings of earlier approaches and attempted to link different theoretical positions. The problem with his concept is the one-sided, Durkheimian emphasis on socialization as a societal process which is most manifestly expressed in the idea of the completed personality as a mirror image of the social structure. Because he concentrates on the mechanism of the internalization of role structures, not enough attention is paid to individuation as an integral component of the socialization process. Socialization is understood only as a process of role acquisitions, in the course of which a member of society gradually learns an increasingly comprehensive repertoire of social skills and abilities that he or she needs to master in order to become a full member of society. Despite his differentiated starting position, this leaves Parsons with a conception of personality formation that places major emphasis on society. Since components of (classical) psychoanalytic theory are only additively included, this emphasis is scarcely corrected. His model confuses socialization with the internalization of social and cultural norms and directs attention away from processes and toward outcomes (Wentworth, 1980, p. 78).

The neglect of individuation and automony that permeates Parsons's theory is caused by the reification of the systems-oriented idea of balance. This is not necessarily due to the systems concept and its theoretical elaboration. The systems concept regards personality, organism, and society as independent systems that reciprocally form environments for each other and interrelate through complex exchange processes. But, because of his strong fixation on mechanisms that stabilize balance, Parsons is inclined to exclude conflicts between the organism and sociocultural expectations of the social system from his analysis. Because of his strong orientation toward the role metaphor, a passive conception of the process of human adaptation to society is dominant. The person is not understood as an active builder and shaper of the environment; rather, he or she faces a highly powerful society whose influences the individual can hardly ward off. To a certain extent, a person's individuality forms itself in spaces that are free from society and distant from socially normed expectations and sanctions.

Parsons underestimates both the scope for the development of an autonomous personality that may deviate from socially established and institutionalized role systems and also the possibility of the existence of value structures and action goals that permit distanced role behavior.

However, Parsons's work also contains some passages that offer a differentiated presentation of the interpenetration of the organic, the personal, and the social system. He often points to the special individuality of each actual person, whose individual socialization and life history lead to a relative independence from social norms (Parsons, 1964, p. 378). But because of the strong fixation of his research interests on the internalization of role structures, he does not manage to integrate this postulate directly and convincingly into his theory and adheres to an "oversocialized" conception of human beings (Wrong, 1961).

Further development of systems theory

Since Parsons's work, many social scientists have attempted to compensate for the mechanistic adaptation slant in his theory. However, one can expect a fruitful further development of Parsons's theoretical approach only if the exchange and interpenetration of the organic, personal, and social systems are precisely worked out and if the potential for tension and conflict that can be found in these exchange relationships is not defined away by oversimplified or reified assumptions of balance. In addition, it is necessary to include the concept of active acquisition and also to systematically realize the individual's conscious reflection on his or her relationship to internal and external reality.

Recently, such a new orientation has been introduced by the extension of systems theory proposed by Luhmann (1984). Like Parsons, Luhmann differentiates between organic, psychological, and social systems. Both the personal and the social system exist in a relationship of reciprocal interpenetration in which the contributions of each are available for the construction of the other. Self-guided consciousness is the contribution of the psychological system that is received by the social system, whereas the social system contributes communication to the construction of the psychological system. For Luhmann, the concept of interpenetration offers the key to a more complete analysis of socialization. It

27

replaces Parsons's theoretical attempts that work with role theory, need concepts, and balance theories. Luhmann uses a terminology that defines socialization with an essentially much stronger reference to self-guided and self-referential mechanisms (Luhmann, 1984, p. 327).

For Luhmann, it is this difference between the psychological system – the person – and its environment – the social system – that provides the possibility and the necessity for socialization. Although in the development of his or her personality a person relies on social actualities, he or she does not become "part" of the social system through socialization. Moreover, society cannot fully control the effects of socialization, because they do not occur in the social system but rather within the person's psychological system. In the interpenetration of social and psychological systems, their diverse elements – on the one side, communication, and on the other, consciousness – act in combination across the system borders. As Luhmann stresses, their self-reproduction as systems with a given structure and complexity thus consists in supplying their elements with the ability to make connections.

Luhmann's theory shows the outline of a modern systems approach to socialization following Parsons. It is obvious that this outline has to be developed in more detail in the future.

Action theory

George Herbert Mead was the founder of a variant of action theory in the American sociophilosophical tradition that has become very influential. Mead's theory is based on openly observable human behavior, but at the same time his analysis essentially concentrates on the subjective and intersubjective interpretation and significance of individual impulses and stimuli and the actions of other persons. The exceptional feature of human behavior, as compared with animal behavior, he argues, is its intentionality and the way in which it is directed at goals. This specific feature justifies the concept of interaction, understood as the sensorially and symbolically interrelated acts of a minimum of two persons. In this approach, action is defined as a sequence of acts that are regulated by the relationships between actors. Action occurs in social situations, is subject to normative regulation, and is in agreement with the actors' motivation. Theories in the social sciences that are based on this concept are generally called either "intersubjective" theories, or "interaction" theories and "action" theories.

Conceptual foundations

In his central work, *Mind, Self and Society* (1934), Mead concentrates on the origin and emergence of human character. The basis for this process, in his view, is human interaction with the natural and social environment. Mead considers human action to be based on physiological and organic conditions, and he analyzes its molding through social interaction processes. Individual and society are conceived as being interwoven and reciprocally determinant in their origins. Socialization and individuation are two interrelated dimensions for Mead, and it is their mutual interplay that makes the emergence of the human subject possible.

In Mead's theory, personality emerges as the product of two quantities: the more social component, "Me," and the more psychological component, "I." The Me presents ideas on how other people view an individual and on how he or she has to behave to meet their expectations. In contrast to the Me, the I possesses a more impulsive and spontaneous quality, which, although restrained by the Me, represents an independent quality of personality. The "Self" emerges as a product of both quantities: the I and the Me. The Self becomes the reflective intelligence of a person and the object of the "Mind." Thus, for Mead, the emergence of the human personality and human action become possible and explicable only through the complex interplay of I, Me, Self, and Mind. The human person is understood as a being with reflexive awareness of itself that constitutes an individual and, at the same time, social subject (Mead, 1934, chapter 32).

Mead places great value on the status of significant symbols that are carriers of meaning for the interaction partners and become carriers of meaning for the self – that is, shared symbols. Significant shared symbols, such as language, in particular, can identify the other's actions and establish relations between the interaction partners. In order to be able to act mutually and in agreement, a person must be able to summon empathy; this means, to estimate the significance of the intended behavior for the other person. This also produces the anticipation of the other person's response.

Each person must see him- or herself through the eyes of the other and anticipate the other's actions as if they were his or her own. Mead regards this internal psychological basic pattern of "role taking" that is developed directly from the interaction as a precondition for every individual action. Each person must see him- or herself through the eyes of important other persons and a collective other person ("generalized others") and in this way become his or her own object, in order to act in a subjectively meaningful manner.

In Mead's theory, social action is understood as a process of symbolically conveyed interaction that takes place through the reciprocal interpretation of definitions of situations, role expectations, and action plans of the partner(s). The perceived intentions and meanings of the other person's actions are, just like the definition of one's own actions, only preliminary interpretations that are continually subject to revision by subsequent events. Interaction is to be seen as a principally open, dynamic, and revisable process that demands constant interpretation and reinterpretation. Despite their generality, societal and cultural value orientations can never offer sufficient behavioral orientations for all potential events. Situations are repeatedly occurring for which no sufficient prefabricated value orientations are available that the person can fall back on. In these cases, behavioral orientations first have to be produced through the common interpretative activity of the actors concerned (Mead, 1934, chapter 38).

Mead's theory is based on a model of a creative and productive individual who processes and shapes his or her environment. The individual is seen as a creative interpreter and constructer of his or her social world. The central quality that liberates the human being from the determinations given by the social and material world is symbolic communication. According to this idea, a person can give meaning to his or her environment and his or her own actions within it. An individual can place him- or herself in the role of the other communication partner(s) who constitute the social environment, and in this way develop consciousness and a self-image. The relations between individual and society are regarded as being dialectical. Societal conditions influence but do not determine human structures of consciousness and action. Human consciousness and human action are not a mechanical expression of social structures. Rather, in this theory, the social structures are formed from the reciprocal interrelationships between persons (Mead, 1934, p. 310). Social structures are the product of the interaction and interpretation of the human subjects.

In Mead's theory, social reality is understood as an interindividual arrangement that is given its particular meaning on each separate occasion. His theory includes the possibility that interactive social structures transform into institutional ones, because the idea of society is linked to the process of communicative action. Society is a collective action that consists of the combining of the actions of all persons who take part in societal life. The linking of individual actions is completed through the process of reciprocal role taking. Social action is made possible by the internalization of societal values and norms, and, vice versa, society changes through the combining of social actions.

Critical assessment

Mead's theory presents a comprehensive sociological concept that permits analysis of the formation and development of the personality within social interaction structures. The theory offers an elaboration of the interactive model of the relation between person and environment. Many ideas that are important for present-day socialization theory were already formulated by Mead, though sometimes in other contexts. His work contains the fundamental idea that each person finds him- or herself in an exchange process with inner and outer reality (cf. Blumer, 1969). The attraction of the theory for socialization research lies in its having aspects of action theory and theory of social structure joined together in a theory of the communicative relationships among persons.

However, Mead's statements on the theory of social structure remain vague. He completely neglects the functional differentiation of complex societies. He does not provide any analytic apparatus for the explanation of power, influence, and conflict in industralized societies. He does not recognize any sociostructural divisions and limitations of action relations in institutional or organizational form. Ultimately Mead was not engaged in a systemic analysis of society but was concerned with the relations between individual action and social processes (Haferkamp, 1984).

31

Social structure and personality development

Mead's work is complex and many-sided. When his work is considered by psychological and sociological authors, often only one out of several lines of theory are taken up and developed further (cf. Joas, 1980). Among psychologists, the social constitution of the personality is often neglected and, among sociologists, the biological and psychological basis.

Theories of social structure

Various branches of theory can be grouped under the term "theories of social structure"; they analyze and interpret the reciprocal relations between the individual and society from the standpoint of macrosocial processes and structures. These theories are based on the contextualistic model but place a much greater emphasis than action theory on the economic, political, and cultural structure of the interrelationships between person and environment. In the view of Jürgen Habermas, who presently is the leading figure in this theoretical tradition, the formation and development of the human personality is placed in close relationship to the development of the social structure of society. The historically concrete totality of a societal life, with its economic, cultural, social, and political processes, is seen as a basis for the analysis of individual development. The central epistemological question is to what degree society's structural and developmental relations permit self-actualization of the person (Habermas, 1970, 1976).

Conceptual foundations

Theories of social structure derive originally from the theory of Karl Marx. For Marx, society is equated with the totality of the material and social relationships that are determined through economic production relationships (Marx, 1844/1966). Modern conceptual approaches have elaborated this early position by introducing a comprehensive materialistic theory of the productive actor who shapes his or her personality in confrontation with societal demands (cf. the review by Ottomeyer, 1980). The most meaningful characteristic feature of the formation of society in the Western world is considered to be (1) the structure of private ownership of the means of production, and (2) the sale of one's own labor power as the characteristic way of earning a living.

According to these theorists, the social and politicoeconomic structures find their expression in everyday activities, have an imprint on everyday social practice, and leave traces in the personality structure of the members of society.

Materialistic theories of personality, as emphasized, for example, in the formulations by Sève (1972) and Leontjev (1964), are based on the early economic and philosophical work of Marx. In his book *Oekonomisch-philosophische Manuskripte* (1844/1966), Marx stressed the reflective and self-objectifying potency of human action. The active and conscious shaping of the objective world was, for Marx, the basis that makes the human being the only conscious species. The human being gains self-awareness in the productive interaction with external nature, in the process of acquisition of the objective world, and at the same time in his or her social relationships with other people. Through the relationship with nature and with one's own species, the individual reflects on him- or herself and forms an awareness of the self. Thus Marx focuses his work predominantly on the production activity of interacting persons, but he, like Mead, recognizes the process of interpersonal exchange of role perspectives.

Materialistic personality theorists deal with the dialectical contradiction that societal factors are, on the one hand, conditions that constitute personality, whereas, on the other hand, the developing personality has to be regarded as an agent that actively changes his or her own living world and the objective environment. They are interested in finding out how a person's own genesis is influenced by the social inheritance, the reality created by others, and how, at the same time, an individual produces this reality through his or her activity as an autonomous human being.

In Leontjev's (1964) approach, the term "activity" becomes the key term for materialistic personality theory. Activities are interrelated chains of human actions that are guided by a motive and aimed at a goal. Behind each motive stands a need. This concept of activity introduces an interesting new category for the analysis of the relations between person and society. It offers fertile conceptual links to action theory.

The theorists of the Frankfurt school also are influenced by the early work of Marx. In recent years, through the decisive influence of Habermas, they have attempted to integrate microsociological theories, particularly interaction theories, into macrotheoretical statements. The breadth of Habermas's work accordingly stretches from (to select two prominent titles) the *Reconstruction of Historical Materialism* (1976) to the *Theory of Communicative Action* (1984).

Habermas's greatest efforts are aimed at providing an analytic apparatus for describing and explaining societal conditions that can assess the degrees of freedom of social action that people possess under different social, economic, and cultural living conditions. Societal conditions and situations should be differentiated according to their repression content, their density of behavioral rules, and the intensity of their behavioral controls. Constellations of social structure are investigated in order to estimate whether they permit interactions and communications that enable each person to develop the necessary skills and abilities for social action (Habermas, 1970). Where situations are predetermined by powerful social structures, persons, or groups of persons, the scope of action is restricted, and unfavorable conditions are present for the construction of action competences.

Habermas orients his theory toward the ideal postulate of "undominated verbal discourse" and thus embeds it in the socio-philosophical tradition. In a pragmatic sense, his theory allows the analysis of structures of social situations according to whether they permit the unfolding of individuals' personal needs and interests and foster a process of identity formation. The theory looks for structural handicaps and possibilities for the unfolding of personal competences under concrete societal conditions (Habermas, 1976, p. 63).

In much of his work, Habermas contributes to a theory that links socialization to the concept of individuation and expressly attempts to combine sociological and psychological traditions of theory for the analysis of personality development. He takes into account action theory and the theory of social structure from the sociological tradition, and psychoanalytic and developmental approaches from the psychological tradition. In this way, he includes a broad range of theoretical approaches. Through his efforts to join together different theoretical traditions in one approach, Habermas emphasizes the need to arrive at complementary approaches in a theory with an interdisciplinary orientation. To this extent, his work represents an attempt to link together similar approaches to developmental and socialization theory and integrate them in a comprehensive concept.

For Habermas, the general goal of the process of personality formation is mastering the rules of reasonable action. If this state of development is given, he talks about the availability of communicative competence. For him, this competence is the ability to produce verbal situations and to participate in them through the mastery of specific verbal acts. A particularly important component of communicative competence is discourse competence – the ability to continuously generate meaning and interpretation through creative argumentative reasoning (Habermas, 1970). According to this conception, an understanding between persons is possible only when a communication situation exists with an undistorted structure of interaction and with equal rights for all participants, so that only the strength of the better argument applies. These conditions for the ideal communication situation are also the prerequisites for the ideal form of living. In this view, the concept of the ideal communication situation anticipates the form of living by which societal relationships should ideally be measured. For Habermas, the ability to take part in discourse is the crucial part of the development of competence that requires the presence of specific cognitive, verbal, interactive, and communicative abilities and skills as preconditions. Specific efforts are directed at analyzing the regularities in the development of communicative competence as the central aspect of research in personality development.

Critical assessment

The positions taken by the various approaches to the theory of social structure provide a much-needed expansion of the theoretical spectrum of socialization theory. Their significance for socialization theory is very great, since they attempt, more intensively than the other theories, to include macrosocial structures in the analysis of the relations between individual and environment. The short sketch that I have just given of the various transformations of social structure theory has shown that all theories from this tradition have moved away in recent years from a one-sided theory of social structure introducing microsociological concepts and by elaborating the notion of individuation.

Habermas is a noticeable example of this. In order to include the rules of human development in his theory, he introduces concepts from developmental theory and action theory into his theory of social structure. The aim of formulating theory in this way is to be able to interrelate statements from theories of social structure, action theory, and personality theory. This provides an ideal theoretical framework for a socialization theory that has to deal with the development of personality in confrontation with social living conditions, and it particularly allows for an understanding of the process of socialization as a developmental process in which competences are built up stage by stage. These competences develop in both concrete historical situations and in the microstructure of their interactive contexts.

Comprehensive approaches of this type bridge the gap between different theoretical traditions in socialization theory. Habermas demonstrates how to combine theoretical concepts in a comprehensive theory that enables us to analyze the conditions required for optimal working of the socialization process.

2

THE INDIVIDUAL AS A PRODUCTIVE PROCESSOR OF INTERNAL AND EXTERNAL REALITY

THE preceding chapter sketched the principal theories that deal with the formation and development of the human personality. As we have seen, depending on the underlying concept of human development and the specific theoretical approach, one arrives at different and, to some extent, irreconcilable theoretical constructions and statements. Each theory addresses specific issues and selects particular topics, which leads to a given concept of personality development. At the same time, several areas of agreement were revealed, particularly in the most recent forms of each theory.

Chapter 1 demonstrated the wide range of epistemological models of human development. As we have noted, the conditions leading to the choice of a particular model as the basis for theory construction and the definition of critical research issues, and for the choice of methodology, are quite hard to define. Historical change, shifts in cultural values and norms, and changes in the philosophical and/or professional standards of the scientific community are just as crucial as personal training and experience and membership in a specific research group. These personal, cultural, professional, and social conditions directly and indirectly affect theory construction.

The process of transforming an epistemological model into a theoretical construct is usually not performed according to criteria that are recognized and shared by all scientists. Rather, typically each group of scientists has specific preferences for certain types of concept formation, conceptual interconnections, and structurings of theoretical statements. Each group also accepts specific criteria for evaluating the quality of the theoretical structure and revising and improving it. In spite of all these factors, we can identify strong forces that are moving toward more inter-disciplinary cooperation in socialization theory.

TOWARD INTERDISCIPLINARY COOPERATION

As we have seen, the most recent variants of the relevant theories are oriented toward an understanding of the reciprocity in the relations between person and environment. There are several important shared qualities that must be elaborated in future theory.

1. All modern theories are turning away from concepts of a linear, single-factor determination of personality development that assume a passively accepted imprinting of the individual by either psychophysical or societal factors. They all, in some respect, share the notion that personality development occurs within the process of an interaction between person and environment in which each individual possesses, applies, and further develops the abilities to acquire, process, manage, and change the social and material reality. They share the assumption that the construction of norms and standards for orientation and behavior occurs as a result of this interaction process, and, at the same time, leads to permanent changes in both personal and environmental features.

2. Modern theories clearly focus on a model of the reciprocal relation between individual and society. This model places the human subject in a social and ecological context that affects the individual but at the same time is always being influenced, changed, and shaped through the individual. This specific epistemological notion of human development will be referred to hereafter as the *model of the productive processing of reality,* in which "productive" is understood as a descriptive concept. The model expresses the common denominator of more recent socialization theories, namely the concept of the individual as dealing with the environment by, on the one hand, searching and sounding out and, on the other hand, constructively intervening and shaping: an individual who perceives environmental facts and relates them to the conceptual structures that are already present, and who is involved in a continual balancing of environmental demands and personal needs, interests, and abilities. The model includes a concept of the (social and material) environment, according to which the environment is in a state of continual reshaping and change and is permanently influenced and altered by the activity of persons.

3. The early socialization research in sociology excluded the "subjective factor" from its analyses or regarded it as only a marginal variable. For a long time this produced a false conception of the process of socialization in scientific discussion. The field of socialization research can be conceived meaningfully only if a linking together of objective and subjective factors is accomplished – in other words, if processes of social institutionalization, on the one hand, and intrapsychological processes of personality structuring on the other are related to one another and linked together. As we saw in our examination of psychological and sociological theories in chapter 1, valuable conceptual approaches have been worked out in these fields that must be included in a comprehensive socialization theory. Sociological and psychological theories are ready for a meaningful completion and interconnection.

An inclusion of concepts from personality and developmental psychology in sociological socialization research, and vice versa, is a necessary but difficult endeavor. For example, in psychology, factors of the social environment are usually taken into account only as marginal variables affecting the individual's psychological functioning. If we want to give them adequate theoretical weight, the concept of person–environment interaction must be transformed in such a way that the social environment is conceived as a constitutive element of personality formation and development, as spelled out in the sociological theories presented in chapter 1. The problem with the sociological theories, on the other hand, lies in their neglect of biological and psychological factors when explaining the social activities of the individual. Whereas psychological theories focus on personality as a dynamic organization of the individual, sociological theories tended for many years to confine themselves to role behavior and situational adaptation and maintained that there was no need for a concept of personality (Geulen and Hurrelmann, 1982).

As we saw clearly in chapter 1, there is no completely satisfactory single theory of socialization, in either sociology or psychology, that can be adopted in its entirety. An adequate theory of socialization must leave room for human autonomy and, at the same time, must acknowledge the existence of patterned social structures that influence individual development. Any comprehensive theory of socialization must express the fact that individuals develop in social contexts and that intraindividual and extraindividual processes are interrelated. Every theory must interconnect several dimensions and levels of analysis, if it aims to meet the requirements imposed by the object of investigation. None of the theories reviewed in chapter 1 is complete. Each is relevant for understanding certain phenomena but tends to ignore other important aspects of human development and social life. As Wentworth (1980) suggests, we need a synthesis of the helpful features of different theories that can be combined into a more complete view of socialization.

The model of the human being as a productive processor and manager of reality is a heuristic projection that does not constitute a specific theory but serves to delineate objectives for theory and research and helps to identify key concepts. In the following sections, this heuristic projection is linked to the contextualistic-interactive model of the relations between the individual and society, reflecting my view that action theory and the theory of social structure present the best prospects for realizing the general theoretical postulates that I have outlined as the goals for future research. I use the model of the individual as a productive processor and manager of reality to serve as a specific illustration of the general model of the interactive relations between the individual and society and as a point of orientation to direct and stimulate theory formation.

The contextualistic-interactive model is particularly suitable as a starting point because it possesses a high power of combining different sources of scientific knowledge and is thus to a large extent capable of integration. In the interactive paradigm, the logical connective laws of both a causal and functional nature that are typical for the mechanistic, the organismic, and the systemic models are included in a more differentiated structure that takes better account of reciprocal relations. Choosing the contextualistic model is therefore not a rejection of the other models but rather a partial recognition of what they are able to provide.

More clearly than the other models, the contextualistic model expresses the specific human form of personality development as a process that is potentially reflexive and self-regulative and that occurs in the social relations between individuals. This model forms the basis for several of the more recent theories advanced in sociological socialization research, such as action theories and theories of social structure that show some convergence in their theoretical statements and, at the same time, some points of agreement with theories of human development coming from the psychological tradition.

As has been shown, the origins of the contextualistic model lie in the comprehensive, expressly interdisciplinary, intersubjective action theory of G. H. Mead (1934). Mead understands personality in a comprehensive sense as the result of an interaction between the individual and the environment that is a process both of socialization and of individuation. What we need, to strengthen this approach, is more theoretical argumentation in the form of bridging concepts that can provide links to both sociological and psychological theories (Geulen, 1977, p. 137; Knorr-Cetina and Cicourel, 1981). As has been pointed out, the theory of communicative action by Habermas (1984) offers important insights. It indicates ways in which action theory, which views individuals as the producers and carriers of social action, can also analyze the features of complex social phenomena that cannot be broken down solely to features of individuals. Obviously, an analysis of complex social structures can be facilitated by extending the frame of reference of action theory beyond the level of the subjective assignment of meaning. Along with Haferkamp (1984), we can postulate that the analysis of fixed social structures and reified systems can be performed more completely by using the theoretical instruments available in micro- and macro-theory.

These are promising avenues for using the interactive model as a starting point for a comprehensive theory that integrates behavioral patterns, at one end of the theoretical spectrum, and phenomena of social structure at the other. Wentworth has suggested ways of translating the contextualistic model into a socialization theory. Unfortunately he adheres to a very narrow definition of socialization as "the activity that confronts and lends structure to the entry of nonmembers into an already existing world" (1980, p. 85). This definition is strongly interlinked with the concepts of social roles of members and novices and the tension between these roles. Therefore, it does not allow us to fully elaborate the potential of micro- and macro-synthesis in interaction theory.

An attempt will now be made to formulate some propositions for a comprehensive socialization theory that makes use of the model of the human being as the productive processor and manager of internal and external reality. The first two are general propositions that will be discussed in some detail here. The six more specific propositions that follow will be taken up again later and elaborated in chapters 3 and 4. I have formulated all of these propositions as hypotheses, in order to show that we are not dealing with a stock of fixed scientific knowledge but with assumptions and postulates that require criticism and discussion. They have some empirical support but are otherwise, of necessity, speculative. I have tried to present them in such a way that supporters of approaches that do not refer to the contextualistic model of person–environment relations will still be able to find points of agreement with their own theories.

Proposition 1

In chapter 1, I defined socialization as *the process of the emergence, formation, and development of the human personality in dependence on and in interaction with the human organism, on the one hand, and the social and material environment on the other hand.* Expanding on this definition, proposition 1 asserts that *the human individual permanently codevelops with cultural and societal factors and builds his or her personality in a process of social interaction.* It assumes that *personality does not form independently from society any of its functions or dimensions but is continuously being shaped, in a concrete, historically conveyed life world, throughout the entire length of the life span.*

Proposition 1 also asserts that *personality development is subject to biological laws that are valid for all human beings.* We have to take into account a high degree of genetic determination of individual variations in personality structures, particularly on some levels of physical structure and physiological functions. The same is true for some levels of intelligence – that is, the ability to learn and profit from experience, to adapt to a changing environment, to motivate oneself to accomplish tasks, and to think and reason abstractly. Biological givens, such as physical characteristics, help determine what development and action potentials are possible. Biological disposition makes an individual a unique physical, psychological, and social being who comes to possess a social stimulus value, evoking differential reactions in his or her interaction partners that influence interactive processes and self-reflective processes (Clausen 1986b, p. 65).

The biosocial character and explanatory basis of human development is generally ignored in sociological concepts of ontogeny. As Featherman and Lerner (1985, p. 660) stress, this exclusion is unfortunate and unnecessary, and it rests in part on a fundamental misreading of theoretical and empirical work concerning human development in psychology, biology, and sociology. As I stressed in chapter 1, human development must be conceived of as a multidimensional but inherently social process at all its levels of manifestation, including the biological. Obviously, it is a characteristic feature of the human nervous and physiological systems to show a genetically determined plasticity that enables the human being to adapt to a wide variety of living conditions.

Thus, the question of whether human development is determined more by the genes or by the environment cannot be answered, simply because the human organism cannot become a person except in a social environment and can develop only in continuous interaction with this environment. The biogenetic vital potentials within the cellular, molecular, and organ systems influence each individual's capacities and performances, but, at the same time, any change in the ecological and social environment has an enormous effect and activates an enormous adaptive potential on the physical, physiological, sensory, cognitive, emotional, and social levels.

The interplay between biological, physiological, and cultural/societal potentials and constraints on the individual can be observed in all phases of life. For example, in all industrialized societies we can identify a biologically determined pubertal change at the onset of adolescence, characterized by a general growth spurt, alterations in facial contours and other body features, and by changes in muscular development, genitalia, and secondary sex characteristics. These events result primarily from an interaction between sex hormones and the cells of the hypothalamus. But in their timing and sequencing, these events are strongly affected by changing cultural and ecological conditions. Over the course of centuries, the onset of puberty has been shown to occur at increasingly earlier ages. In 1860 the average age for the onset of puberty in girls in the United States was 16.5 years, but today it is 12.5 years. This finding must be attributed to changes in social and ecological living conditions, cultural lifestyles, and particularly to changes in nutrition (Hamburg and Hamburg, 1975). This example shows that not only can biological factors influence features of human development but that, at the same time, cultural factors can influence biological processes.

Proposition 2

Proposition 2 asserts that *the theoretical analysis of personality development requires the construction of specific analytic categories for understanding the reciprocal relationships between the individual and society.* In some respects, it is necessary to isolate central units of analysis, although one should bear in mind that the central focus of analysis remains the complex reciprocal relations among these units. Of course, such an analytic method runs the risk of these scientifically constructed units becoming self-determining and then to some extent being treated as representations of reality. This danger can be avoided only if these concepts are an integrated part of a comprehensive theory of socialization.

Conceptually formulated units of analysis have the function of differentiating among related phenomena that are considered essential for analysis. Analytic units can be differentiated according to their degree of complexity and their wealth of features and functions. Their differentiation is particularly helpful if processes and structures that belong together according to one particular theoretical perspective can be combined on the level of concepts. In this sense, units or levels of analysis are understood as components of a complex entirety in which each level of analysis represents relevant conditions for the others (Geulen and Hurrelmann, 1982, p. 52).

The individual as processor of reality

Most of the theoretical constructions in the field of developmental psychology and sociological socialization research that have been mentioned use three central units of analysis:

1. *Social and material environment.* This unit covers all the actualities of a person's material and social surroundings and living conditions that lie outside the organism and thus form the "external reality."

2. *Human organism.* This unit covers the basic genetic disposition, the physiological structures and processes, and the basic physical features of an individual person and thus form the "internal reality."

3. *Personality or personality structure.* This unit is understood as a person's particular organized structure of motives, attributes, traits, attitudes, and action competences. Personality is gained through interaction and communication with persons and objects of the social and material environment and is based on the structures of the organism. Personality, in other words, is the result of the processing and managing of external reality (environment) and internal reality (organism) at all points in time during the life span.

As has been said, during the process of socialization both environment and organism have to be perceived, acquired, processed, and managed. This process leads to a *subjective representation* of sections of the environment and sections of the organism. Personality development thus occurs in a permanent process of reciprocity between two independent and, at the same time, interdependent realities.

If we consider the earlier theoretical concepts, it becomes clear that the approaches that belong more especially to the psychological tradition concentrate on the analysis of the interrelationships between internal reality and personality development, whereas the approaches that lean more strongly toward the sociological tradition are more involved with the relation between personality development and external reality. This difference in emphasis is in line with the historically developed and effective demarcations (in the sense of a satisfactory division of labor) between psychology and sociology. This division of labor, however, must not be permitted to lead to a differentiation in emphasis that blanks out a comprehensive view. Since the disciplinary origins of scientists who work in the fields of developmental and socialization theory

45

will, even in the future, retain a discipline-related theoretical focus, it is necessary to undertake theory formulation in such a way that it is open and receptive to the different theoretical emphasis of its neighbor discipline.

I am convinced that the orientation toward the contextualistic model is particularly helpful in providing the necessary understanding of theoretical concepts and constructions beyond each discipline's own borders. The metaphorical character of the epistemological model of the individual as a productive processor and manager of reality can be seen to encourage cooperation between different disciplines, since it manifests shared references and stimulates a unified application of terms.

Let us turn now to the more specific theoretical propositions.

Proposition 3

Proposition 3 asserts that *in order to analyze socialization as a processing of external reality, it is necessary to carry out a systematic investigation into the nature of social and material living conditions.* The historically developed social structure of a society, the value system, the organized societal subsystems of politics, production, labor, administration, welfare, religion, and social control, as well as the organized medical, psychological, and educational facilities, and the informal groups that are directly relevant for socialization (family, peer group, neighbors, circle of friends, and so forth) affect the formation of the concrete social and material actualities and situations with which each person enters into an (inter-)active exchange. This exchange, which is a process of acquiring and processing external reality, essentially takes place through social interaction and communication with other persons (Berger and Luckmann, 1967). The structures, values, and norms that are significant for society find expression in the structure of this interaction and communication. For example, families and peer groups function as relatively autonomous mediators for the processing of external reality, but at the same time they are related to all the other societal subsystems that in turn have a strong influence on their potential for development and action (Clausen, 1968; Inkeles, 1968, p. 103).

Socialization theory thus has to begin with an analysis of the historically developing economic, political, social, and cultural structures of a society. It has to take into account the historical process of differentiation in the functional areas of society that has led to a removal of educational and socialization functions from the family and to the establishment of an autonomous societal subsystem for education. Socialization theory, in this understanding, has to deal with the functional problems of educational institutions and must also include all the other societal institutions that are relevant to socialization. This is necessary because, despite the historically documented increasing concentration of educational functions in specialized subsystems such as nurseries, schools, vocational colleges, universities, and so forth, there is an ever wider distribution of influences affecting the different institutions and organizations of a society that are relevant for socialization – especially since the spread of the mass media.

Proposition 4

Proposition 4 asserts that *by given conditions that are subject to historical change, the process of acquiring and processing external reality takes place in mainly face-to-face social interactions within families, peer groups, and other informal social institutions.* These face-to-face groups document specific forms and styles of acquiring and processing external reality in their structure of interaction and communication that are based on the previous and present experiences of their members. These styles express the person- and group-specific forms of interaction with external reality and, at the same time, the previous history of this interaction. In this way, families and other institutions that are relevant for socialization provide specific modes of interpretation and problem-solving strategies for interaction with the social and material environment that are adopted in an individually modified form by their members. To the same extent as adults, children and adolescents should be understood as group members who, through their interaction processes, participate in the shaping of their own development and personality formation in an interactive context (Gecas, 1981; House, 1981).

Proposition 5

Proposition 5 asserts that *with progressive personality development in childhood and adolescence, a person's ability to acquire and process reality expands continuously, so that the person arrives at a growing individual understanding of external reality, a more complex cognitive map of his or her physical and social world, and a more effective mastery of biological needs and psychological motives. In this way, an increasing ability to structure and direct personal behavior is achieved* (Brim and Kagan, 1980; Flavell and Ross, 1981).

With progressive personality development, each individual builds up personal structures of strategies for balancing between internal needs and external expectations (as a rule, with little awareness of the process by which this comes about); constructs a knowledge system of experiences and rules; and further develops this system in a flexible manner throughout the whole of life. The basic structures of this system are formed during childhood and adolescence, and, in this respect, these phases of life differ qualitatively from the ones that follow. The basic verbal and interactive competences and the ability to consciously reflect on one's personal process of development are, usually, fully available by the end of the adolescent phase. Each new life situation and each new type of life event, in the later phases of life, place correspondingly altered situative and general demands on personal abilities to cope with tasks, solve problems, and organize personal behavior (Newman and Newman, 1975; Lerner and Spanier, 1980; Hurrelmann, Rosewitz, and Wolf, 1985, p. 17; Clausen, 1986b, p. 88).

In all modern societies, age has become an important organizing and sequencing feature of the life course. Chronological age regulates the movement of individuals through their lives in terms of structuring educational and occupational career pathways for entry into or exclusion from cultural and social participation. It is characteristic of industrialized societies to have a tripartition of the life course into a phase of preparation, one of economic activity in the occupational system, and one of retirement (Clausen, 1986b; Kohli, 1986). These mechanisms for institutionalizing the life course function as background forces and reference points for personal orientation. Modern societies, however, show a low degree of consistency of social demands over time and situations, and that is the reason why modern individuals have to develop and maintain highly adaptive and flexible capacities for self-regulation.

Proposition 6

Proposition 6 asserts that *in spite of biological determination and the cultural constraints mentioned, personality formation and personality development must be conceived of as processes whose outcome and results can, within certain limits, be influenced by a person during all phases of his or her life course.* The organization of behavior in the process of development can be understood as a *process of self-regulation through feedback.* Lerner and Busch-Rossnagel (1981) and Haan (1981) have expressed this pictorially in their metaphor of "individuals as producers of their development." As a rule, a person is oriented toward future development, which, in turn, represents the result of previous interactions with social expectations, biological prerequisites, and personal desires and requirements. If a person perceives deviations from the respective stage of development that is fixed by expectations of social reference groups, he or she will attempt to counter them with a series of self-regulated interventions. These have the goal of bringing about changes in internal conditions or external contexts that promise to have the potential of leading to the intended changes in the state of development (Silbereisen and Eyferth, 1986, p. 9).

Self-regulation of action during the life course should, accordingly, be regarded as a central mechanism for the formation of the personality. Each person has to develop the ability to cope in a suitable manner with different "developmental tasks" that occur, according to age and/or situation. The mastering of new developmental plans should, when possible, occur when the major subproblems involved in previously followed plans in the personal development have been solved. If this is not successful, the self-regulating ability can collapse, and control over the results of interventions in personal development can be lost (Havighurst, 1972; Clausen, 1975; J. C. Coleman, 1980).

The mastering of developmental plans depends on the formation and development of a person's "action competences." "Action," in the strict sense of the word, can be understood as a specific subcategory of behavior, namely (at least to some extent) as *goal-directed and intentional behavior.* By the word "intentional," we mean that the objective performance of the action is linked to subjective experiences and that these are accessible to the actor: The action is cognitively represented. As von Cranach and his coworkers have stressed, we cannot expect that all actions and their components are correctly represented. Further, we cannot expect that all components of actions are conscious. Conscious representation can, for example, be restricted to the beginning, end, or specific salient phases of actions (von Cranach, Kalbermatten, Indermühle, and Gugler, 1982, p. 24). Thus the specific features of "action" cause it to stand out from behavior that is the totality of all human activities including unconscious, unplanned, and reactive forms, although in the actual course of events action is mixed repeatedly with these other forms.

Special forms of action that are of great importance for personality development are *interactive* and *communicative action*. Broadly speaking, interaction describes those forms of human behavior that feature reciprocal influences. If these interactive actions are oriented toward a common symbolic (verbal, mimic) comprehension pattern, and if an interrelated exchange of information and meaning occurs, then they fulfill the criterion for communicative action (Habermas, 1970).

The competence to act and, in particular, the competence for interactive and communicative action are prerequisites for a person's being able to manage the demands and requirements of everyday situations in the span of the life course. But competence for action can be effective only if it takes into account and introduces a person's own motivations, needs, and interests. The processing and managing of reality is, as previously mentioned, a process that is aimed in two directions: inward and outward. In the course of personality formation, action competences are constructed for interaction with external and internal reality.

Proposition 7

Proposition 7 asserts that *in order to process and manage external and internal reality effectively, a person needs a self-concept. The concept or image of the self is an internal conception of the entirety of motives, attitudes, and properties, and action competences, as well as an evaluation of them, and that a person gains when looking at his or her own activities. A self-concept that is not only realistic but at the same time offers a sense of "identity" must be regarded as the prerequisite for the ability to act flexibly and competently in the course of life.*

50

"Identity" here means the continuity of self-experience on the basis of the self-concept.

A continuity of self-experience can be developed when an individual possesses the competence to balance "internal" needs and "external" expectations. A person is better able to form a stable identity the more abilities he or she possesses for coping with personal biological and psychological dispositions, the more autonomously the person moves through the social environment, the more he or she is embedded in a secure structure of social relations within the social network, and the more the person receives recognition from the social environment in important societal role connections. Identity also possesses a life-historical component: the experience of an unchanging self in the course of passing through different phases of life, developmental tasks, and life events (Cottrell, 1969, p. 551). It would appear that under present conditions, the formation and maintainance of a continuity of self-experience is more difficult than it was one or two generations ago, because social roles and situations are subjected to rapid change.

Proposition 8

Proposition 8 asserts that *whether or not socialization is successful is decided according to how suitable the individual action competences, the self-image, and the identity formation are for the developmental tasks in a given biographical and social situation. If the structure and profile of the behavioral repertoire are not sufficiently developed, there is a risk that psychologically and socially deviant forms of action and behavior will arise that bring about problems for the further development of the personality.* Deviant and problem behavior are essentially based on a lack of agreement between the action competences that a person has developed (which are the result of an internal balancing of motives, needs, interests, and environmental expectations) and the forms of action that are demanded in actual life situations. Thus, deviant and problem behaviors are indicators of environmental structures that do not permit the personality to unfold according to the person's needs, motives, and interests.

From the perspective of socialization theory, careful attention must be paid to social resources as well as personal resources for coping with environmental demands. Social resources place a person in a position to interact competently with specific situational demands. The social and material living conditions make available a more or less suitable supportive potential for a person's action performance. Each person is bound to a network of social relationships that can offer support when coping with problem constellations.

The goal of social and educational interventions that can be derived from socialization theory must, accordingly, be to place a person in a position in which he or she can in some way cope with the behavioral demands of the situation and that opens up new possibilities for personality development. This requires, on the one hand, a change in the social, institutional, and/or organizationally structured profile of demands and, on the other hand, an improvement in individual abilities and skills (Gottlieb, 1983; Pearlin, 1983; Hurrelmann, Kaufmann, and Lösel, 1987).

PROPOSITIONS CONCERNING METHODOLOGY

Now that we have examined the theoretical consequences that the model of the productive processing of reality has for socialization research, we shall briefly consider the methodological consequences. It is possible to derive methodological and not just theoretical considerations from each of the four models of the relationships between the person and the environment that were defined in chapter 1. Each model leads to different methodological statements and procedures. These particularly differ in their assumptions about the possibility of empirically assessing and recording social reality, the degree of standardization for research instruments, and the degree to which the research findings can be generalized.

During the last 20 years, several different conceptions of methodological procedure have been discussed that refer to the various epistemological models. "Positivistic" positions that align research in the social sciences with the standards of natural science generally correspond to the mechanistic model of personality development. Using strictly controlled measurement, subject to standardized conditions with highly experimental designs, specific and mostly predefined assumptions are tested in order to produce a systematic investigation of social actualities and their causes. Methods for analyzing the research findings are also strongly oriented toward natural-science standards and favor analyses that permit the tracing of data relations back to causal structures and the reporting of dependencies between cause and effect with the highest possible level of quantification (Lazarsfeld and Rosenberg, 1955).

The opposite pole is occupied by the methodology that corresponds with action theory in the contextualistic model. This tends more toward a "phenomenological" position: The aim of the application of methodological procedures here is to achieve better understanding of social actions of individuals in realistic social constellations through the use of holistically oriented observation and questioning for recording data. Therefore the analysis of the recorded data concentrates primarily on describing and reconstructing subjective interpretations of the persons under investigation, in order to trace the relationships between actions and their social context (Bogdan and Tayor, 1975).

Between these two methodological positions, other interesting variants of empirical recording methods and data analysis have been developed within the traditions of the organismic and systemic models. One can name, for example, the clinical methodology of psychoanalysis, the quasi-experimental recording and interview methods of cognitive developmental theory, the naturalistic-ecological methods of field observation in ecological developmental psychology, and the structurally oriented macroanalysis of the materialistic theory of personality.

The contrasts between the various methodological positions have been unnecessarily exaggerated in the literature for many years. This has led to the impression that even in the practical research process one is dealing with mutually exclusive procedures that are a consequence of completely different processes of scientific working. The investigations that are oriented at one of the extreme poles of methodological procedure, however, are well known for their limits: In the positivistic tradition, the continual refining of recording methods, the permanent raising of the level of standardization, and the search for isolable effects of single variables (the so-called quantitative methodology) have neglected the holistic nature of variable structures in personality research. On the other hand, the phenomenologically oriented ("qualitative") case-study methodologies have often made it impossible to analyze the structural relations among individual variables and generalize them to theoretically relevant hypotheses.

It would therefore seem to be best to reflect on the origins of empirical research in the social sciences, to test out the methodological positions therein, and in future to proceed increasingly with combinations of both procedures: Along with "qualitative" survey procedures that take into account a great number of variables and their interplay in one and the same investigation, one should simultaneously undertake "qualitative" holistic, case-related analyses, in order to balance the pros and cons of both methodological procedures. With this approach, the different methodological foundations of the various empirical recording and evaluation procedures will not be denied or blurred, but the pragmatically meaningful possibilities of supplementing both procedures will be fully exploited.

The habit of turning single methodological procedures into absolutes is, in my estimation, at least partially due to the pervasive neglect of theoretical guidance and control in empirical assessment. Theory formation and methodological procedures have gone their many separate ways and do not always coexist in a fruitful symbiosis. A purposeful choice of designs and procedures of empirical investigation must be based on a theoretical definition of the problem or area of research to be investigated, with reference to the underlying epistemological model. Data collection methods and data analysis procedures must be subordinated to theory formation. They have secondary significance in the research process and should never be allowed to become autonomous and, from such a position, influence or dictate the theoretical starting point.

In order to improve and further develop the range of methods, it is necessary to assess the epistemological worth of the various methodological procedures realistically, in an unconditional and open manner. There has been a growth of readiness to do this among all groups of scientists, regardless of their theoretical or methodological background. We can see here a process of development similar to that noted for theory development: Although the orientation toward the epistemological model has a fundamental influence on the choice of methods of data collection and data analysis, it does not make it impossible for different groups of researchers who refer to different epistemological models to cooperate with one another.

Despite certain reservations, the model of the productive processing of reality is a highly suitable orientation for the choice of methods in socialization research. It can serve as a focal point for different lines of research methodology, because it allows for different causal, functional, and interactive relationships among variables. In the next section I will present some propositions that result from using the model of the productive processing of reality as an orientation for data collection and data analysis. These propositions again are presented as hypotheses and are given in an open form, so that they contain as many points of connection as possible for the supporters of other methodologies.

Proposition 1

Proposition 1 asserts that *the heuristic model of the individual as a productive processor of reality must be transformed by methodological procedures that are capable of linking investigations of the historically developed structuring of external reality with investigations of subjective perceptions, interpretations, and processings of external reality and then analyzing this link in a methodologically controlled way.*

As a researcher, I can understand the individual only when I project him or her into a social and material context, when I imagine the person interacting with this context and then work out which opportunities this individual has for subjective interpretations, actions, and developments and which of these he or she realizes. An analysis of the objective social world in which the individual lives is a necessary supplement to the investigations of the subjective structuring of the meaning of the social world. Only when I consider both, can I, as a researcher, relate objectively and subjectively perceived possibilities and alternatives to one another and obtain indications about the status of subjective interpretations of reality, relate the problem-solving capacity to the subjectively perceived situative context, and outline the consequences of successful or unsuccessful attempts at solving problems (Hurrelmann, 1985).

For the transformation into the research process, this means that macroanalytic and microanalytic levels of analysis have to be interrelated, while taking account of their reciprocal influences on one another. As long as no better procedures are available, we must try to manage with the available methodological tools for recording changes in features of society and personality and their links to one another. This means that procedures for the analysis and interpretation of both social structures and personal structures must be included in the research process.

Proposition 2

Proposition 2 asserts that *as long as the unit of investigation is the individual person, it is important for the data collection procedure to look for a way of getting at the desired information by recording information through both self-observation by the person and observation by others, including the scientific researcher.*

Information about the life history, personal experiences, and personal features and characteristics can, to a certain extent, be collected only from the report of the persons concerned. Thus, a methodologically controlled procedure that records the results of self-observation by questionnaire, interview, diary, and so forth represents the only practicable way. The communication and recording of self-observation can follow a written or verbal, and an open or standardized, form.

The procedure of self-observation is methodologically limited by differences and restrictions in ability to recall information, the inadquate possibility of training personal observation, by systematic errors of estimation and judgment, and distortions of perception by personal needs. The information about an individual gained from a person through self-observation is also hard for the scientist to validate. For example, in the research area of parent–child interaction, it has been repeatedly demonstrated that mothers' retrospective reports on such matters as the age at which they had weaned or toilet-trained their children are highly inaccurate, although there are some items of information for which later reports match concurrent reports fairly well. As Maccoby and Martin (1984, p. 17) have pointed out, there seems to be no general principle that would distinguish retrospective reports that can be relied on from those that cannot. They therefore stress the need to use more concurrent instead of retrospective reports of subjects as informants: To move farther in the direction of obtaining information that is highly accessible to parents because of its recency, daily report instruments have been developed, usually using a checklist that is based on telephone interviews in which the parent is asked to report which child behavior has occurred within the last 24 hours. A similar technique is to use parents' daily diaries or parents' accurate description of recent events.

Because of limitations of self-observation and self-report methods, it is necessary to supplement this procedure with observational methods: "Observers may be trained to be reliable recorders of carefully specified behavioral events, using uniform comparison standards. When all of the children in a particular study are observed under constant circumstances and with uniform coding criteria, sources of variation in child behavior resulting from the observational situation or variously defined coding categories can be minimized" (Maccoby and Martin, 1984, p. 18). However, as the same authors point out, observational methods may provide researchers with a false sense of objectivity: The representativeness and ecological validity of the conditions of observation deserve serious consideration.

As a consequence, it appears that some sorts of information can more reliably be obtained from one type of method than the other. Given the strengths and weaknesses of any single method, it is desirable to use a mixture of methods. This technique has been defined as "triangulation," in the sense of a "combination of methodologies in the study of the same phenomenon" (Denzin, 1978, p. 291). The triangulation metaphor is derived from navigational strategies that use multiple reference points to locate the exact position of an object. The convergence between two methods is considered to enhance the belief of the researcher that the results are valid and not a methodological artifact:

> Parents may be interviewed, or given questionnaires or Q-sorts to complete; children may be included as informants via paper-and-pencil tests or interviews; and parents and children may be observed both together and separately in both naturalistic settings and the laboratory. In a sense, such an approach amounts to "covering one's bets": To the extent that distortions and incorrect inferences are drawn from any single data source such problems can be minimized by using several data sources. (Maccoby and Martin, 1984, p. 24)

Thus, by using multimethod designs, distortions and one-sided processing of information can be avoided or balanced out. Only with a combination of different procedures is it possible to arrive at a reconstruction of the person's social relationships, subjective patterns of interpretation, and styles of processing the social and material environment.

Proposition 3

Proposition 3 asserts that *for an effective investigational design, a combination of standardized and nonstandardized recording procedures, as well as a combination of quantitative and qualitative analysis procedures, are particularly useful.*

As a rule, a combination of survey and case study designs is to be recommended. Large samples of persons can be investigated with standardized procedures such as fully structured questionnaires, whereas an intensive case study procedure using participant observation of an unstructured type can be based on a limited subpopulation either simultaneously or as a supplementary procedure. Such mixed research designs allow, on the one hand, a representative and statistically certified overview of the distribution of important variables, and, on the other hand, a holistic description of the connections and the structure of relations among different variables. Whereas case studies permit a more detailed testing of which situations and events correspond with which patterns of processing and forms of action, survey studies make it possible to estimate the status of these findings in a total population and to state the frequencies of occurrence and the distribution.

Qualitative "fieldwork" methods of a nonstandardized type, which usually are applied within case study designs or very small samples, can play a prominent role by eliciting data and suggesting interpretations and conclusions to which other methods would be blind. The idea of triangulation can be applied again at this methodological level: The weakness of each single research design can possibly be compensated for by the counterbalancing strength of another. That is, it is assumed that the survey design does not share the same weaknesses or potential for bias as the case study design, and vice versa. The linkage of both types or designs is supposed to exploit the assets and neutralize, rather than compound, the liabilities (Jick, 1979, p. 604). Researchers using qualitative methodology (that is, preferring case studies with nonstandardized fieldwork methods) should be encouraged in addition to utilize sampling techniques, to develop quantifiable schemes for coding complex data sets, and to systematize their observations. Conversely, quantitatively oriented researchers (preferring survey studies with standardized questionnaires and interviews) should be encouraged to select subsamples for the purpose of semistructured, probing interviews of an explorative nature (Sieber, 1973). Qualitative designs play an important part in triangulation:

> The researcher is likely to sustain a profitable closeness to the situation which allows greater sensitivity to the multiple sources of data. . . . In one respect, qualitative data are used as the critical counterpoint to quantitative methods. In another respect, the analysis benefits from the perceptions drawn from personal experiences and first hand observations. . . . Finally, the convergent approach utilizes qualitative methods to illuminate behavior in contexts where situational factors play a prominent role. In sum, triangulation, which prominently involves qualitative methods, can potentially generate what anthropologists call "holistic work" or "thick description." (Jick, 1979, p. 609)

Proposition 4

Proposition 4 asserts that *for better methodological safeguarding of socialization research, it is necessary to combine both cross-sectional and longitudinal procedures in the experimental design.*

Cross-sectional analyses depict only momentary recordings of relations among variables and have little to say about the development of a person or a group of people over time. In order to increase their meaningfulness, it is first necessary to try to carry out a follow-up investigation after a set period of time. In this way, it is possible to gain indications of changes in relations among variables over time, although the population is a different one at each point of data collection. Second, an attempt can be made to include retrospective assessment elements in cross-sectional analyses: The results of the analysis can be supplemented by indicators from the previous biography that can be related to the actual situation. Such a procedure works with objective data from previous phases of life that can be obtained from documents such as the person's school and hospital records. In this way, despite the limitations of a cross-sectional procedure, it is possible to reconstruct the earlier biography and important living conditions and relate these to an individual's personality features and actual behavior. Besides documentation, it is also possible to fall back on the recall procedure, in which subjectively remembered data take the place of objective data from past life. Naturally, this latter procedure is much more open to distortions than the former.

Thus it can be seen that there are operative steps by which cross-sectional studies can be improved, so that they provide some indicators for the analysis of personality development. However, such methods do not enable us to obtain methodologically satisfactory findings for the analysis of the processes of change in personality features that correspond to social changes. Reliable statements on this are provided only by the panel design, namely, the longitudinal study (Nesselroade and Baltes, 1979). This commences with persons or groups of persons who are characterized by a distinctive feature. These people are investigated again, at regular time intervals, in order to relate behavioral findings at later times to the originally recorded criteria and features. Parallel to this, an analysis of the social environment and its structural conditions must be carried out at each time of recording. This procedure requires considerable time and effort, but it provides the opportunity of systematically plotting the development of a person or group of persons, explaining changes in features and forms of action and simultaneously including in the analysis the conditions of development and their outcomes. This is the most effective procedure for recording covariations between societal and personal conditions (Nesselroade and van Eye, 1985).

In the coming years, socialization research will have to invest much energy in developing a suitable methodology. It proves to be extremely difficult to carry out in a methodologically controlled manner investigations of societal and social structures that include the interaction structures that are relevant for socialization research and at the same time undertake investigations into the individuals' interpretations of these objective actualities. As has been shown, the necessary methodological implications can be recognized only when qualitative-interpretative procedures of data collection and data analysis are applied alongside quantitative-statistical ones, case analyses alongside survey analyses, and longitudinal studies alongside cross-sectional ones (Hurrelmann and Ulich, 1982).

An excellent example of a multimethod design, which combines survey and case studies and is carried out in a longitudinal procedure, is the Longitudinal Research Project, undertaken by the Institute of Human Development of the University of California at Berkeley. The Guidance Study was initiated in 1928 with 248 boys and girls. Half of the cases were designed to be experimental subjects whose parents received guidance in child care, and the other half served as controls. The Berkeley Growth Study was a much more circumscribed study of mental, motor, and physical development in infancy, entailing frequent observation and testing in the early months of life, using a subsample of 60 children who were born in the same time period as that covered by the Guidance Study. Finally, the Oakland Growth Study was initiated in 1931–2 to examine the social, intellectual, and physiological development of a cross-section of boys and girls from preadolescence through the high-school years. The sample of over 200 boys and girls ranged in age from 10 to 12 at graduation from five Oakland elementary schools. Today, the Institute of Human Development has secured data from nearly 300 study members of all three samples, who now range in age from 55 to 65. The special value of the data available at the institute is that the staff have used observations, interviews, questionnaires, and tests, including multiple respondents, and that they have combined survey and case studies. The results of the Berkeley studies cover a wide spectrum of variables that are of special importance for the analysis of biological and social conditions for successful socialization across the life span (Clausen, 1986a; Eichhorn, Clausen, Haan, Honzik, and Mussen, 1984).

3

SOCIETAL CONTEXTS OF PERSONALITY DEVELOPMENT

HOW can we picture the societal contexts of personality formation and development? In this chapter, using three of the propositions for a comprehensive socialization theory described in chapter 2 (propositions 3, 4, and 5), we will examine possible ways of estimating the effects of the social structure of society on socialization.

The essence of the three propositions is as follows:

- *Proposition 3:* In order to analyze socialization as a processing of external reality, it is necessary to carry out a systematic investigation into the nature of social and material living conditions. Socialization theory thus has to begin with an analysis of the historically developed economic, political, social, and cultural structures of a society.
- *Proposition 4:* The process of acquiring and processing external reality takes place mainly in face-to-face interactions within families, peer groups, and other informal social institutions. In this way, families and other institutions provide specific modes of interpretation and problem-solving strategies for interaction with the social and material environment, which are adopted in an individually modified form by their members.
- *Proposition 5:* With progressive personality development, an increasing ability to structure and direct personal behavior is achieved. Modern societies are characterized by age-specific regulation of the movements of individuals through their life course. At the same time, however, modern societies show a low degree of consistency of social demands over time and situations, and therefore modern individuals have to develop and maintain a high level of adaptive and flexible self-regulation capacities.

As has been stressed in the propositions, the medium of socialization is concrete social interaction. The content of this interaction is shaped by the social structure of the environment. This social structure displays the fundamental norms, standards, and cultural designs of the society and reflects the distribution of political and economic resources. The most relevant social settings for socialization are organized in specific social contexts. As Wentworth defines it, these institutionalized and organized contexts represent the social order and are the units of the culture presented to the individual. Societal contexts can be conceived of as a situation- and time-bounded arena of human activity relevant for the process of socialization (Wentworth, 1980, p. 92). In this respect, the concept of societal context is a unifying link between the analytic categories of micro- and macro-analysis used in this book.

In this chapter we shall examine each of these propositions in turn. The first section analyzes formally organized societal contexts of personality development. These contexts contain a miniature social world, while drawing upon the larger societal world for cultural content and legitimation. In the next section we turn to an informally organized context of great importance for socialization – the family. One focus of this section is the question of how the different living, working, and learning conditions of the members of the family affect the process of socialization. Without doubt, the family retains its key role in personality formation and development, despite changes that have occurred in the nature of the family over the course of history. The last section is concerned with the importance of educational and occupational career patterns in the life course, and the structures and processes of socialization in adulthood.

THE INFLUENCES OF FORMALLY ORGANIZED SOCIALIZATION CONTEXTS

The relationships between economic, political, cultural, and social power within a society determine that which, at any concrete historical point in time, scientific discourse calls the "social structure" of the society. The concept of social structure covers

1. The degree and form of the *division of labor* among subgroups of the population, social institutions, and organizations
2. The degree and form of *equality or inequality* in the societal distribution of resources such as power, influence, prestige, income, property, and education

Social structure and personality development

The social structure of a society has a tremendous influence on the composition of the social and material living conditions in which the members of society find themselves. The social structure determines that which becomes the external reality for an individual and is therefore of direct relevance for socialization.

We will first look at the aspect of the societal division of labor. The social structure of industrial societies has undergone considerable change in the last few decades. This change has taken the direction of a growing division of labor among societal institutions and organizations through increasing specialization of specific tasks and functions. The differentiation of the social structure in which separable functions are bound to specific subsystems is typical for the present formation of industrialized Western societies.

Typical for present-day societies are specialized subsystems of economy, politics, administration, social control, religion, health services, welfare, psychosocial care, science, education, and information. Most of these societal subsystems are drawn up in the form of large social organizations (e.g., factories, offices, corporations) that operate according to their own specific rules and regulations. In the course of historical development, new fields of work and demands on societal reproduction have led to the continual formation of new subsystems. This process of the differentiation of specific subsystems of society that represent separate areas of life for its members is a process that is still continuing today (Habermas, 1976, p. 129; Luhmann, 1982).

The relevance of societal organizations for socialization

One of the consequences of this process of differentiation is that each member of society has to deal daily with a large number of institutions and organizations and must come to terms with their respective behavioral demands throughout life. This requires very specific action competences, with a high degree of situational and contextual flexibility, that have to be developed during the course of personality formation. (I will deal with this field in more detail in chapter 4.)

However, a consequence of this differentiation process is also that each member of society is daily and throughout life exposed to the influences of a great variety of institutions and organizations – influences that can leave important traces in the personality. Each single organized societal subsystem is responsible for the shaping of the direct situative and social actualities of its members or clients. In its own specific form, each subsystem influences the possible ways of structuring the process by which its members or clients individually cope with external reality and is therefore relevant for socialization.

Repeated attempts have been made to assess and differentiate the organized societal subsystems according to their degree of relevance for socialization. The differentiation between organizational tasks that relate to the processing and transformation of objects and those that are directed at the influencing and processing of persons ("subjects") has proved to be of little value. Recent research into the way that "object-transforming organizations" in the fields of work and production function has made it clear that their relevance for socialization is as high as that of "person-processing organizations": For the production of objects, one requires a number of people who are involved in this process and who have reached an agreement about how to do it. The subsequent changes in personal attitudes, expectations, and actions are highly significant for the development of personality (Kohn and Schooler, 1983).

A classification according to object-related and subject-related organizational tasks alone can provide little information about the relevance of an organized societal subsystem to socialization. It would appear that the intensity and duration of a person's links with an organization are more important criteria. An organization's relevance for socialization can be regarded as being particularly high if the organization enlists persons as members, clients, inmates, or participants with a correspondingly defined social status, because this status requires at least a partial transfer of organizational demands and behavioral expectations to the person. Different grades of influence on the development of personality result, depending on the degree of commitment and the duration of the association.

In the field of "person-processing" organizations, there is no doubt that institutions that enlist persons as members, clients, or inmates for long periods of time with the goal of influencing personality are highly relevant for socialization (Brim and Wheeler, 1966, p. 59). Examples of this are psychosocial care establishments (psychotherapeutic institutions, inpatient and outpatient psychiatric treatment centers, and other therapeutic and rehabilitative institutions); social-educational establishments (children's homes, educational and youth counseling agencies); youth work establishments (vocational training programs, employment programs); and criminal justice establishments (residential houses, prisons). A special case, which will not be dealt with here, is establishments for military national service and their civil alternative for conscientious objectors.

These establishments are characterized by the dominance of the goal of altering personality in their official organizational purpose, external presentation, and in the consciousness of their professional staff. They are mostly committed to tasks involving control, intervention, and rehabilitation policies. In carrying out these tasks, they influence the personality development of their clients and inmates. Their major concern is the handling of social or psychological problems, the control of deviant behavior, and the compensation of developmental deficits. This work is generally carried out through direct personal contact between professional staff and clients or inmates (Goffman, 1961; Plake, 1981).

It is hard to estimate the relevance to socialization of another group of organizations of increasing significance, such as political parties, clubs, citizens' groups, trade unions, and professional organizations. These organizations enlist persons as members in order to attain either personal or collective goals that are concerned with influencing the external social or material reality of a society. Their members have to make at least a partial adjustment of attitudes, expectations, and actions in line with the purpose of the organization, and this adaptation has repercussions for personality development. The forms of commitment and cooperation that these organizations demand can thus lead to personal dispositions that have lasting effects on individual features and traits.

It is also difficult to estimate the status of the mass media of information and entertainment in the socialization process. These differ from organizations just discussed in that they address their message to a public who are neither members or clients but, as a rule, anonymous. This public is not incorporated into an organized membership system or any other binding form of lasting cooperation. The organizational purpose of the mass media lies in informing and entertaining all members of society, not a section of society that is defined or excluded by specific criteria. This is yet another way in which the mass media differ from the other previously discussed organizations that are relevant for socialization. The effectiveness of mass media for personality development strongly depends on the form and intensity of their integration into the social context of family, peer groups, and the immediate social environment in which they are received. The everyday patterns of interaction decide the potential effects of the media and also the evaluation and interpretation of their messages (Schorb, Mohn, and Theunert, 1980; Gurevitch, Bennett, Curran, and Woolacott, 1982).

Because of wide-ranging new developments in the fields of information and communication technology, it can be predicted that the mass media will further increase in significance in the daily life of people in all phases of life. Many people already live in an environment that is strongly influenced by media such as radio, television, video, disco, movies, and electronic games. As the working week becomes increasingly shorter in all industrial societies and the commitment of adults to work-related production and service processes decreases, at least in terms of the amount of time involved, it is probable that the mass media will become even more important. The mass media have become an integral part of the social and material living conditions in modern industrial societies, yet, at the same time, they function as a mediator of external reality to a nonspecific public. In principle, this double role in the process of socialization also applies for the other subsystems mentioned, but its influence through the mass media is especially comprehensive. The mass media permeate all the other social organizations and structures of a society, whereas the remaining subsystems are generally restricted to a specific, limited area of influence.

The status of organized educational establishments

In the course of the differentiation of the social structure and the development of organized subsystems, specialized educational establishments have formed. They belong to societal organizations that have undergone a particularly rapid expansion during the last two to three decades. Increasingly, all educational procedures and education-related activities have become concentrated in preschool institutions, schools, vocational centers, and universities (Archer, 1979).

If we look at the strong dynamics of this process, we can say that the industrial societies find themselves on a path toward a societally planned and organized education. This is, first, because the proportion of those interactive processes that affect the construction of the sociocultural personality of the members of society is increasingly being carried out by educators who are formally engaged as professionals and controlled by society in purposely developed complex organizations. And second, because the proportion of the population in industrial societies that is involved in organized educational establishments such as kindergartens, preschools, schools, vocational establishments, and universities is increasing from decade to decade (Coleman, 1982; Meyer and Rowan, 1983).

The causes of this developmental process lie in the societal changes that result from the interplay of conditions of economic production and political power structures. The increasing complexity of industrial development makes it functionally necessary to transfer education to a separate subsystem of society. The economic growth and political stability that are important foundations of societal survival are becoming more and more dependent on the availability, application, and evaluation of knowledge and intelligence. The educational system attains an outstanding significance for their development and dissemination (Hurrelmann, 1975, p. 45; Bourdieu and Passeron, 1977).

The increase in field of activity and responsibility of the state makes it possible, and at the same time necessary, to include the educational system in its comprehensive task of securing economic growth and political stability. State-controlled educational policies are continually expanding. Examples of this are preschool education and postschool vocational training. Both areas were, until only a few decades ago, predominantly the concern of the family system or the occupational system but are now increasingly coming under the control and guidance of the state (Carnoy and Levin, 1985, p. 49).

For the field of economic action, the organized educational system is expected not only to deliver a sufficient number of graduates to the occupational system, at specific times, but also to adequately train these graduates. This means to prepare them for the existing patterns of economic order and to train them specifically as a potential work force. Because the technical and organizational foundations of production and service procedures are constantly changing, abstract basic qualifications such as flexibility and adaptability have to be trained (Carnoy and Levin, 1985, p. 114). The educational organizations are expected not only to equip the future work force with the instrumental and cognitive abilities that are requested by the occupational system but also to foster the ability to learn and adapt, and to construct the necessary social and psychological attitudes and behavioral dispositions.

The organized educational establishments are, without doubt, highly relevant for socialization. Their main organizational goal is to train intelligence, reasoning skills, knowledge, and social values, through the planned and precisely steered actions of professional staff, but their actual influence goes far beyond these cognitive dimensions of the personality of their clients and affects emotional and social dimensions as well. This influencing is brought about through direct social contact between educators and clients (children, trainees, students, etc.) that is structured by the organizational features of the educational institution (Bidwell, 1965; Kerckhoff and Corwin, 1981).

A characteristic feature of the structure of interaction and communication in educational establishments is an asymmetrical relationship between the interaction partners. Because of their societally ordained and organizationally fixed professional status, educators are in a superior position to shape situations and the course of interactions. Despite this asymmetrical structure, the actual "educational work" on the personality development of children and adolescents is a mutual and reciprocal process. Each educator observes the behavior of the children and adolescents through the filter of his or her own perception, which involves specific personal assumptions, attitudes, and experiences. These perceptions are categorized and interpreted in a way that is specific to the personality of the particular educator. As clients of the organization, the children and adolescents, in turn, see the educator's action through a filter of their own perceptions, which leads to responses to and the initiation of new actions. These actions are, in turn, perceived by the educator as feedback to his or her own actions, so that a continual dynamic interaction of

69

reciprocal influences is brought about (Hurrelmann, 1975, p. 191; Gecas, 1981, p. 178).

The precision and sensitivity of their reciprocal perceptions and reactions to the actions of the other in this role structure are crucial for the educational success of the institution. Educators, on the one hand, and children and adolescents on the other, are representatives of complementary social roles, form different definitions of the situation that are linked to their role positions, and interpret and evaluate these roles in different ways. An important component of educational work is the reciprocal assessment and coordination of these different definitions of situations, attitudes, and behavior dispositions.

Through their educational work, the organized educational establishments convey a specific form of adaptation to and interaction with social and material living conditions that strongly depends on the particular organizational nature of the establishment. Not only are the intended and planned educational activities that are documented in organizational statutes and curricula and in the subjective intentions of the educators relevant for socialization, but so also are the institutional and organizational influences in themselves, because they permeate the form of interaction between educators and students. The interaction and communication structures that are formed between educators and students contain specific stimuli and indications for the students' acquisition of externality (Heyns, 1978).

Through their educational work, the educational institutions function as a transfer medium for the impulses and demands of the social and material environment. In this way children and adolescents acquire specific patterns of perception and specific forms of processing and coping with external reality. They are prepared for those competences that are important for life in society as seen through the eyes of the educational institution. In this way, the educational institutions work as conveyers of external reality and offer assistance in the adaptations and acquisitions that are directly significant for personality development. They do this in an intensive and concentrated form, so that, compared with the other societal subsystems, they exert a strong influence on the development of personality.

Educational organizations are social contexts with a double function: They are mediators of the environment and, at the same time, they are a part of their clients' external reality. Because of the great extent to which they push their way into the forefront of everyday life, they become the crucial component of external reality in childhood and adolescence (Hurrelmann, Rosewitz, and Wolf, 1985, p. 79; Hurrelmann, 1987a). Their influence on the development of personality qualifies the influence of the other organized societal contexts of production, politics, welfare, social control, psychosocial care, and mass media.

The influence of all the contexts combined represents a differentiated mixture of various offers and demands that, in the end, have to be processed individually by each individual person. The contexts form a concrete web of living conditions that is the object of individual acquisition and processing. In this connection, the educational organizations take on a key role, since the declared goal of their organization is the coordination of the various influences. Schools should systematically build up the central components of the perception and interpretation of external reality in its political, economic, cultural, and natural manifestations. They should involve children and adolescents in productive interaction with reality and encourage them in this interaction process. The same applies to the other educational organizations. Organized educational contexts should offer orientations for the acquisition of and confrontation with external reality. As we have stressed, they can fulfill these mediatory functions only within the framework of the given organizational structure – with all the limitations and restrictions that this necessarily involves (Rutter, Maugham, Mortimore, Ouston, and Smith, 1979).

A structural model of the contexts of socialization

The sociostructural influences of organized societal contexts on the formation and development of personality are, as we have just seen, difficult to estimate. The various organized societal subsystems differ in their relevance for socialization, since they create different conditions for the acquisition of and interaction with external reality and mostly contain organization-specific proposals for the mediation of external reality. The different subsystems are intertwined in a complex manner, so that their demands and proposals overlap with and influence one another. They function with and alongside one another, according to each system's specific stipulations (Geulen and Hurrelmann, 1982, p. 58).

In childhood, there is, for example, an overlapping of variously organized child-minding relationships and forms of care for small children. A mixture of kindergarten or day nursery, neighborhood help, and maybe even parent–child groups and the support of relatives, as well as family care, is typical for the individual child. Formally organized, semiformal, informal, and familial forms of education thus may complement one another (Borman, 1982). Even if the general trend in all industrialized societies is toward a strengthening of the proportion of formal forms, the other forms are usually still retained and determine the everyday conditions of socialization (Bronfenbrenner, 1978; Clausen, 1986b, p. 79). No child can be considered as receiving only one kind of child care. Even the child who spends the whole day at a day nursery is still also cared for within the family. As a rule, the forms of child minding alter according to the time of day. The number of persons with whom the child has a close relationship, their age, sex, education, and life background, and also the form and style of social contact, type of relationships with peers, material and social stimuli, and so forth, alter with these changing forms of care. At the same time, the specific given conditions for the development of personal features and traits also alter.

The same applies for other phases of life. In the adolescent phase, for example, it is typically schools, vocational establishments, youth clubs, peer groups, and religious and political associations that exist alongside one another as important contexts of socialization. Here too, we have to reckon with specific effects whose influences overlap (Hurrelmann, Rosewitz, and Wolf, 1985, p. 70).

The family context has a key role in the process of socialization. The family's status in the life course has altered considerably, as a consequence of the historical changes mentioned at the beginning of this section. However, under today's conditions, the family is still the most decisive and, in terms of temporal duration and intensity, the most important social institution for the process of socialization in childhood. This is because, as in a microcosm, the family context reflects the material and social living conditions that are conveyed through the interaction of parents and children from the earliest phases of childhood.

A way of combining the most important societal institutions and organizations into a structural model of the contexts of socialization, taking these various considerations into account, has been demonstrated by Dieter Geulen and myself (Geulen and Hurrelmann, 1982, p. 57). Figure 3.1 illustrates this idea. The model includes the general economic, technological, political,

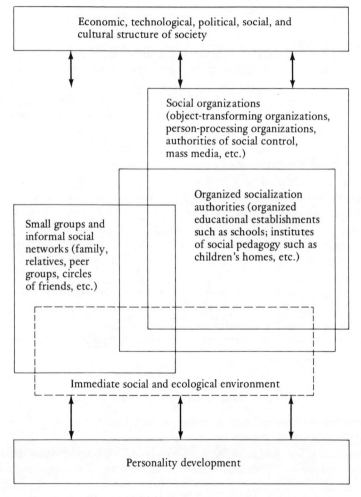

Figure 3.1. Model of the structure of socialization contexts.

73

social, and cultural structure of the given, historically developed society. The institutionalized and organized contexts of socialization have been differentiated into small groups and informal social networks, organized socialization authorities, and other social organizations.

SOCIAL INEQUALITY, LIVING CONDITIONS, AND FAMILIAL SOCIALIZATION

In this section we will examine the aspects of equality and inequality in social and material living conditions, and their importance for familial socialization. The distribution of power, influence, prestige, income, property, and education in a society has both indirect and partially direct influences on the process of socialization, because, to a considerable extent, this distribution determines the nature of the social and material living conditions with which persons have to interact. The distribution of material and immaterial resources in all industrialized societies is characterized by a high degree of inequality. The distribution structures remain quite stable from one generation to the next. There is a strong possibility that the reproduction of inequality is largely owing to the education and socialization functions of the family. Experience shows that many of the dimensions of the family's position in the social structure are handed down to the next generation.

What do we know about the relations between a family's social and material life situation, the familial socialization, and the children's personality formation, and how do these relations affect the position of the younger members of the family in the social structure?

The hypothesis of class-specific socialization

The "class-specific socialization research" of the 1960s and 1970s, which was based on analytic classification models of social inequality, investigated the ways in which living conditions influence features of personality and contribute to a reproduction of inequality in social structures (cf. Bronfenbrenner, 1958; Hoffman, 1963; Kohn, 1969; Bernstein, 1971; Kerckhoff, 1972). The basic theoretical assumption is that the family is a social micro-cosm of society that hands down the basic values of society to the following generation and thus determines the children's scholastic achievements and scholastic records, as well as their future occupational careers. In this sense, social inequality is "socially inherited" by the next generation, and we can say that the process of socialization takes a circular course. This hypothesis can be illustrated graphically (Figure 3.2). As the figure shows, this model

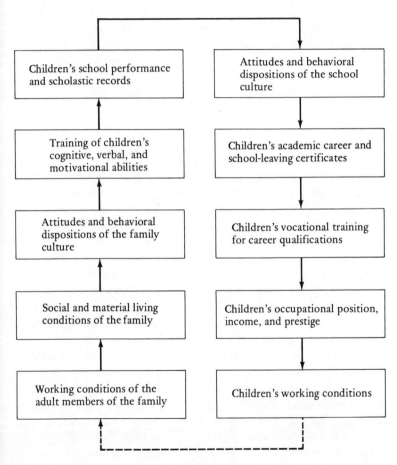

Figure 3.2. Graphic presentation of the class-specific socialization hypothesis: the "circular course" taken by the process of socialization.

proposes a direct relation between the social and material living conditions of the parents, the development of the child's personality, and the social career of the child in school and occupation.

This hypothesis requires some critical analysis. The class-specific hypothesis assumes a strong influence of early childhood, parallel to the assumption of a high level of stability across time, in the vocational and social structures of society. These assumptions are difficult to prove (cf. last section of this chapter). Second, the hypothesis is based on research findings that, although they provide only limited evidence, are frequently overgeneralized and declared to possess general validity. The restrictions that limit empirical studies in this field were often overlooked or covered up. As a rule, the empirical investigations available assess only specific aspects of the relations among the variables included in Figure 3.2. Thus, the hypothesis concerning the "circular course" of the socialization process must be understood as a heuristically valuable theoretical assumption that can give rise to new hypotheses in the future, but it must not be regarded as an exact description of reality. It cannot be proved empirically in the form in which it is presented here. It would be possible to test the circularity relation only within the framework of a long-term study stretching across generations (Bertram, 1981, p. 27).

The class-specific socialization hypothesis has led to an overinterpretation of the available research findings on the relation between vocational group membership and parents' educational behavior, on the one hand, and children's personality features on the other. This overinterpretation is related to the scientific and political expectations with which socialization research was confronted during the 1960s and 1970s. In the scientific and public discussion of the time, the predominant opinion was that in working-class families the individual ability of a child was not satisfactorily developed through the specific educational practices of the parents, so that these children lived in a situation of cultural deprivation and had to face disadvantages in their educational and occupational carreers (Persell, 1977). This assumption enjoyed wide political support and had a decisive influence on the demands placed on research into education and socialization.

The circularity hypothesis received so much attention because it provided a plausible explanation for the low level of school success of working-class children. Because of the strong political interest in explanations that could also provide a basis for action strategies, the unproved and hypothetical character of these statements was overlooked. Frequently scientists also did not distance themselves sufficiently from the generalizations and reifications of these hypotheses that were carried out in political fields (Hurrelmann, 1975, p. 115).

The hypothesis of class-specific socialization, in spite of all the criticism, has provided further stimulus for the use of more precise methods to investigate the relations among social strata, socialization, personality features, and the biography, and also for more carefully applied interpretations of research findings. It focuses on a scientific and political problem that is as crucial today as in the past and that requires the concentrated attention of socialization theory and research. The basis of further analyses, however, should no longer be the class concept but the concept of living conditions.

Social and material living conditions and personality formation

In sociological research, the terms "social stratum" and "social class" are used to describe a subgroup of society whose members possess specific shared features and differ from other subgroups according to their position in the social structure. Such concepts are mostly based on a ranking model. The term "class" implies the concept of a series of layers, in the sense of a hierarchical ranking of population groups of different status with horizontal demarcations (Dahrendorf, 1959).

In the research approaches of the 1960s and 1970s, the determination of the social class of members of a family was generally based only on the profession of the father. The justification given for this was that the vocational position of the father permitted a ranking of the family according to the dimensions of income, prestige, and influence, and indirectly, the dimensions of education, power, and property as well. In the controversial discussion of the findings from class-specific socialization research, both supporters and opponents of this procedure have often overlooked the fact that the formation of classes can be only an analytic and methodological aid for the analysis of social structure.

Social structure and personality development

Social classes are artificial constructions introduced by the researcher, rather than phenomena that can be recognized and differentiated in reality (Persell, 1984, p. 246). They serve to classify similar constellations of social and material living conditions in the continuum of social inequality. Persons who are assigned to a social class or social stratum do not "belong" to this class or stratum but are assigned by the researcher to a constructed social unit for the purpose of identification and analysis. Thus, social classes are always only abstractions from the complexity of societal reality. Material and immaterial resources such as power, property, income, prestige, education, and so forth, are, in general, distributed across a continuum in a society, and they can be brought into classification only for analytic and theoretical purposes, either singly or in combination.

An attempt to classify social and material living conditions can be of use only if it is guided by theoretical considerations and by theoretically relevant target parameters. Socialization research therefore requires a range of instruments for classifying living conditions that is both as highly differentiated as possible, and, at the same time, precise. The exact form of these research instruments has to fit the actual object of investigation and, in addition, be adjusted according to the concrete historical constellation. It is highly unlikely that a range of instruments exists that is meaningful in each historical constellation and for every chosen object of research.

If we wish to achieve a more accurate specification of living conditions, it is indispensable that we use a wider range of indicators of a family's social and material position and do not just record the occupational position of father and/or mother. Such indicators include those just mentioned (income, property, education, power, influence) and also "ecological" factors such as the characteristics of the place of residence, the service infrastructure of the residential area, and the quality of the family home and its size, as well as the social origins and cultural traditions of the parent's families of origin. To some extent, these factors mutually influence one another and occur in specific constellations that have to be recognized in their respective typical clusters.

Thus, in order to leave behind simplistic class-analytic constructions, in the future preference should be given to differentiating and classifying specific sets of social living conditions. The identification of these sets must include a wide range of indicators, in order to obtain a broad and differentiated spectrum of determining factors. Sets of living conditions that are identical are characterized by a specific combination of manifestations of all of these indicators. For socialization research, it is of particular importance to investigate how persons with the same or different sets of living conditions perceive and interpret their life situation, so that we can reach conclusions about the subjective forms and mechanisms of the processing and managing of reality. In the next section, we will examine some prominent examples of this type of research.

The significance of occupational experiences

In order to be able to describe and explain the social and material living conditions of a family more exactly, some recent investigations have attempted to analyze what effect the working conditions of adult members of the family have on their personality development. According to these studies, it is vocational and occupational conditions that are decisive for personality development, because they determine the degree of the practice of self-determination at work that also transfers to the nonoccupational field: Positive occupational conditions encourage a positive opinion of self and society, which, in turn, encourages a belief in the possibility of rational and goal-oriented action and increases the valuation of self-determination. Negative conditions of vocational life lead to a narrowly restricted image of self and society and acquiescence to authority. The most important conditions are those that are decisive for the degree of self-determination that a person can enjoy in his or her work: no strict supervision, complex work content, and a nonroutine working day (Kohn, 1969; Kohn and Schooler, 1983, p. 103, p. 125).

According to this research, the substantive complexity of one's work is causally related not only to values, self-concepts, and social orientation but particularly to the powerlessness, normlessness, and self-estrangement components of alienation. People who do complex work come to exercise their intellectual capacities not only on the job but also in their nonoccupational life and value self-direction more highly than those who do repetitive work. Thus, complex work leads to seeing the entire social world as being complex and as offering alternatives and choices. This world view facilitates personal planning, encourages personal activities, and develops the sense that problems are manageable and solvable; it thus helps to overcome alienation and to develop a strong sense of coherence (Antonovsky, 1979). This allows for a high capacity to cope with stressful situations in everyday life and to solve social conflicts and tensions, and it helps to provide a life experience that has personal meanings and makes sense to the individual and gives the feeling that participation in determining the outcome of everyday conflicts and tensions is possible.

Kohn and his associates find some evidence that parents introduce the value orientations that they have developed at work into the familial educational process. Parents educate their children for the world that they themselves experience at work. In this way, the children are prepared for the value orientations and life-styles on which their parents depend: conformist ideas, in working-class families, with an emphasis on external influences and consequences, and, in families in advantageous life situations, autonomous ideas, with a stress on self-guidance.

Kohn's investigations are convincing to the extent that they point out relations between vocational experiences and personality features, in particular value orientations, among the occupationally active members of the family. His assumption of a direct relation between the parents' work-related value orientations and their ideas about education, however, still has to be proved. Although it is plausible to assume that through their educational behavior parents hand down to their children those attitudes and behavioral expectancies that are of particular significance for their own range of experiences, Kohn's studies do not yet show how these transfer mechanisms work. The empirical relations between vocational group membership and various educational orientations are constant and consistent, but they are weak. Although the relation between working conditions and the personality features of adults is very strong, vocational group membership explains a variance of only about 12 percent of the educationally relevant value orientations of parents (Abrahams and Sommerkorn, 1976; Gecas, 1979).

Thus, Kohn's investigations have drawn attention to the high status of occupational experiences for the formation of parental personality but do not provide empirically satisfying proof of the effects of parental educational orientations and behaviors in the familial system of interactions. The educational attitudes and – even more important – the actual educational actions of the parents are the result of the complex interrelated activities of *all* the members of the family. Since Kohn's studies, there can be no doubt about the key role of vocationally determined work actualities for parental value orientations, yet this factor should not be regarded in isolation.

The significance of the familial role structure

In several of the more recent studies that followed the work of Kohn, an attempt has been made to assess the intervening and moderating variables that lie between social and material living conditions (including working conditions) and educational orientations and practices. These studies are based on the assumption that work experiences and the material and social living conditions of the members of the family find expression in the role structure, and the corresponding interaction and communication structures, of the family. In these studies, the familial role system is assigned the function of mediating between the working and life experiences of the parents, on the one side, and the children's personality formation on the other.

Bernstein was one of the first socialization theorists to develop a category system that differentiates among the parents' living conditions, familial role structures, and personality features of the children, thus including three levels of analysis. Bernstein develops typologies to characterize different familial role structures. He particularly differentiates them according to whether the behavioral scope of the members of the family is fixed by their social status (mother, father, son, daughter), which he calls "closed structure," or whether they are flexibly negotiated by specific personal features ("open structure"). According to his studies, a closed structure is more frequently found in families in which the parents have to face restrictive work experiences, and an open structure is made possible through autonomous work experiences. The open role structure corresponds to a system of interaction and communication in the family that is flexible and oriented toward the individual persons, and the closed structure is a rigid one that is oriented toward the status positions of the members of the family (Bernstein, 1975).

Different forms of social control, and thus the influencing of the children's forms of behavior, correspond with these communication systems. Thus, in person-oriented families social control is carried out through elaborate verbalization, and in status-oriented families through restricted verbalization. The language and speech development of the children, which functions as a bridge for the development of cognitive and intellectual abilities, is influenced by these different strategies of social control in the family context (Bernstein, 1975, chapter 6).

Bernstein's specific research interest is directed at the analysis of symbolic systems that he understands as regulators for the individual acquisition of the structure of societal relationships. By "symbolic systems," he means the language patterns and speech modes of the members of the family. The various social conditions and rules that predominate, depending on the family's life situation, also lead to different ways of using the rule system of language. The language patterns and speech modes are a reflection of specific social and material living conditions. Through the language patterns, the social structure of the society influences the structure of life experiences, the access to societal knowledge, and the structure of communication. Elaborate language patterns and speech modes give a person access to a representation of the societal order and the structure of social interaction in which he or she lives. On the other hand, restricted patterns considerably limit such access (Bernstein, 1971, chapter 2; Swanson, 1974).

According to this approach, both the different experiences of work and social and material living conditions are transformed into specific social life situations that not only influence the personality features of the individual members of the family but also determine the structure of interaction and the communication structure of the family as a social system. The larger the area of alternatives for the verbal realization of various meanings that the interaction structure permits, the more individualized the possibilities of verbal expression, and the more flexible the choice of syntax and vocabulary. According to Bernstein, it is person-oriented interaction structures that facilitate and encourage an elaboration of verbal patterns and thus provide generally favorable preconditions for the construction of the competences of social action. Figure 3.3 presents, in an idealized form, a graphical illustration of Bernstein's explanatory model.

In this explanatory model, parental attitudes toward education and the parents' educational practice are given the theoretical status that is appropriate to them: They are an expression of the parents' processing of the social and material living conditions (external reality) that are reflected in the interaction structure of the family. Because it makes allowance for the interaction level, Bernstein's approach has brought a considerable advance in understanding, in spite of the simple theoretical construct that he uses and the inadequate empirical substantiation of his assumptions. His approach has made us aware that the development of children's and adolescents' personality features in families should be seen to have a close relation to the family's interaction and communication structure.

A central finding from the research stimulated by Bernstein is that familial interaction and communication systems contain a specific symbolic coding of the environmental experiences of the members of the family. This coding documents the family-specific style of processing external reality (the social and material living conditions). The familial system of interaction and communication, in each case, makes specific cognitive, emotional, and social categorization and problem-solving programs available for coping with the social and material environment. Although the mechanisms by which language patterns and speech modes affect personality development are not always clearly elaborated in Bernstein's work, the general tendency of his statements has frequently been proved in follow-up studies (Gecas, 1979).

It is important to keep in mind the ideal-type construction of Bernstein's model. Empirical reality, of course, is far more complex and inconsistent than the model: Parents may have restricted work experiences without having unfavorable living conditions; parents may have conformist value orientations but, because of the influence of relatives and other significant reference persons, be committed to the idea that their children should experience as much intellectual and social stimulation as possible in kindergarten and school, and so forth (cf. the results of the longitudinal case studies of parents' orientations and commitments by Clausen, 1986a). Bernstein's model, however, is of great heuristic value, because it outlines particular socialization influences that

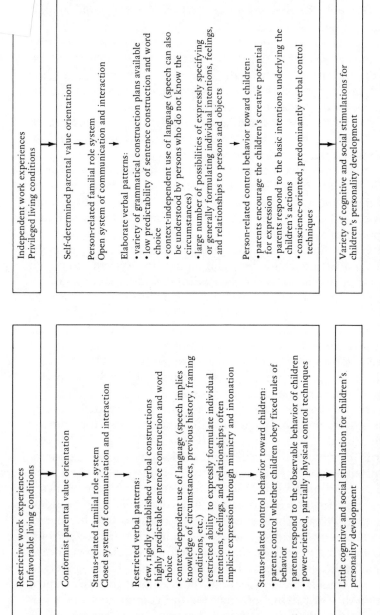

Figure 3.3. Bernstein's model of relations among working conditions, familial role structures, verbal patterns, parental control techniques, and children's personality development.

explain a theoretically very important part of the variance in the total personality development of children.

Current investigations into familial socialization

Ideas taken from this research tradition have been adopted and extended in more recent psychological and sociological investigations into familial socialization. The central goal of the newer research is to study the environment of the family with respect to the quality of conditions for the children's development. Following the ideas of Bronfenbrenner (1979), an investigation is made of the social and ecological properties of the family environment, with its differing potentials for stimulation, support, strain, and stress.

As we can learn from these studies (e.g., the collections of research papers by Laosa and Sigel, 1982; Sigel and Laosa, 1983; Schneewind, Beckmann, and Engfer, 1983), the family environment must be understood as the potential field of experience of its members. The particular experiences of each individual member of the family influence the interaction events within the family. These interaction events, in turn, present the medium for the children's development. Although the material and social environment of the family determines the quality and breadth of the child's potential learning and social experiences, the parents serve as mediators of the environment in the "deciphering" of external reality by prestructuring the actual fields of experience. The way and form in which this occurs mainly depend on the parents' educational style, the relationship between the marriage partners, and the general family climate (Schneewind et al., 1983, p. 30).

The key feature of these contextualistic and ecological research approaches is that they understand the entire structure of relationships (on which the parents' educational style is based) as a transfer medium for socialization. It is not the influence of a single factor that is regarded as being significant for children's personality development but the network of relations among a variety of factors. These approaches make us aware of the combined effects of different factors in the social and material living conditions and clearly show that the effect of a single factor depends on its relation to other factors. The social and material living conditions appear as a closely woven structure of conditions that supply a living space for groups and individuals. This living space can be classified as being either more, or less, stimulating and supportive for the child's personality development.

In this sense, we see that the goal of class-specific socialization research is being picked up again, but this time within a more flexible theoretical and empirical framework. Modern ecological and contextualistic approaches to family research no longer employ a one-dimensional concept of class as a qualifying variable for the status of a person or family but favor a multidimensional conception of social and ecological living conditions. They pay particular attention to ecological factors, in addition to aspects of the hierarchical, social, and economic inequalities mentioned earlier. It has yet to be proved whether this expansion of the spectrum of indicators provides an empirically more satisfying explanation of the mechanisms and processes of the relation between social actualities and individual features (Bertram, 1981, p. 147). *There are some indications that socioeconomic and socioecological effects are closely linked, so that the inclusion of ecological variables does not open up a totally new quality of theoretical explanation but only completes the circle of independent variables in the research process.*

The transformation of living conditions into personality features follows complex, multicausal lines of influence that are affected by reciprocal monitoring processes. It would appear that constellations of variables exist that take effect only through the mediation of specific moderating and intervening variables. The most important of those intervening variables are the network of social support, and the personal processing and coping strategies: Specific unfavorable living conditions have an unfavorable effect on personality development only if support or coping strategies either fail or are insufficient (this idea will be further elaborated in chapter 4).

Future research needs

The studies on the relationship of living conditions and familial socialization summarized here have provided important new findings and insights. Future research should focus on some very important thematic aspects that have been somewhat neglected and that must be taken into consideration if we are to provide a complete picture of familial socialization.

Societal contexts of personality development

1. *More thorough investigations into the role-specific influences of mothers and fathers on the socialization process are needed.* There are a great number of studies of the mother–child relationship, but they usually do not take into consideration the social and material living conditions of the family and do not investigate the maternal and paternal role in the familial education process in a separate and differentiated manner. The findings from research up to now have shown that the mothers' value orientations for educational activities are influenced by the (working) fathers. It is argued that the men supply the family with material resources (income) and immaterial resources (prestige, status) and that this influences the women's attitudes and behavior within the family (Steinkamp, 1980, p. 279).

Future research must investigate whether this assumption actually holds. In order to do this, the work and life experiences outside the family of both fathers *and* mothers must be included. One of the most conspicuous deficits of past studies is that they disregard the significance of the mother's gainful employment. Although the traditional pattern of work distribution in the family, in which the man goes to work and the woman is concerned with the home and children, is increasingly a thing of the past, we still have little certain knowledge about the effects of these changes on the children's socialization process. Studies by Kohn and Schooler (1983, p. 195) have shown that working experiences affect women's personalities in the same way as they affect men's personalities. However, the question that concerns us is whether the traditional ideas about the roles of men and women affect how these experiences at work are transferred to the familial interaction. It is likely that even working women are deeply involved in housekeeping and child rearing, so that their professional experiences may often receive less weight within the family than the man's, who still has the traditional role of the breadwinner of the family.

This raises the question of what effect the father/man has on the childhood socialization process. If we look at this from a purely temporal perspective, most fathers are much less involved with their children than mothers. In her study of preschool children, Engelbert (1986) found that mothers are by far a child's most important contact person: On average, mothers spent 206 minutes with their child each day, whereas the comparable value for men was only 31 minutes. This picture does not change much as the children grow older. This low temporal engagement of fathers does not definitively show whether the quality and intensity of the relationship is also correspondingly low. The available studies point to the important function of fathers as models for the children's (in particular boys') cognitions and intellectual development, but there are as yet no clear results on the effects in the emotional and moral-ethical field (Lamb, 1976; Fthenakis, 1985, p. 290).

2. *Studies that precisely plot the actual structure of relationships in a family, as well as the dynamics of interaction and communication, are needed.* Only by referring to actual everyday familial situations is it possible to analyze how parents give their time and attention to the needs and desires of their children; how they solve conflicts with their children; what are the temporal, spatial, and material limitations on shared action; what value orientations are actually involved in the interaction with the children; or to what degree children have opportunities to influence the shaping of the interaction. This list presents only a few of the important questions and dimensions that have scarcely been researched.

Valuable indications are provided here by case studies that have been carried out mostly on the basis of observations or interaction protocols. They permit the identification of repeated patterns of parental behavior that recur during everyday interactions between parents and children and that can be shown to influence the pattern of the children's behavior. These case studies complement the interview-based studies referred to earlier with analyses of situation-related parental behavior that is relevant to education (Hess and Handel, 1959; Denzin, 1977; Garbarino, 1982).

Such case studies clarify the family's own dynamics and the relative autonomy from the external world that it achieves as an interaction system, while recognizing that environmental factors influence the interaction and communication structure of the family. It is through the form of interaction with the environment that is typical for the family that a part of this environment becomes the family's life world. The studies show how the social filtering processes work that decide to what extent and in what way the environment leaves its mark on familial relationships and, vice versa, how familial relationships influence the environment. The autonomy is relative, not absolute. The scope for decisions and actions is (pre-)structured by the socioeconomic and socioecological placement of the family. Its independence as a dynamic interaction and communication system is limited by these macrostructural conditions. However, within these limits there is a varied flexibility in the social, cultural, and communicative shaping of the relationships among the members of the family. The biography of each individual member sets specific and unique accents on the contacts among all members, and the history of the whole family as a system influences the style and form, as well as the structure and content, of the relationships among the members.

An important task for future research is to provide a precise analysis of the interaction processes that are relevant for socialization. Parental attitudes and educational practices could prove to be important factors, but it would seem that the concrete features of the interaction process are important: the structural and regulated form of the social interaction; the motives and intentions of the interaction partners; the respective possibilities for influencing the definition of the situation; as well as the affective quality of the relationships with interaction partners (Damon, 1977; Doise and Palmonari, 1984). Research based on accurate reconstruction and observation of the social relationships between parents and children and the parents' educational activities gives evidence that high parental demand, consistent parental discipline, authoritative rather than permissive educational style, flexible and reciprocal communication between parents and children, and emotional acceptance and warmth on both sides, particularly the parents' side – that is, parents acting on a high level of educational competence – produce competent children in adolescence (Baumrind, 1978; Clausen, 1986a; Mortimer, Lawrence, and Kumka, 1986).

When we consider the child as an individual who productively processes reality and introduces his or her own interests, we cannot anticipate a mechanical transformation of features of the interaction structure into psychological features. Values, norms, and situational interpretations are conveyed and transformed, but which of them is internalized by a child and become relevant for action, and how this occurs, is a subject for future research. Moreover, it is important to clarify which of a child's or an adolescent's personality dimensions is more strongly or weakly accessible and/or exposed to social influences such as socioeconomic and socioecological actualities, and what significance these influences have in the total structure of the developing personality.

3. *Future investigations should pay more attention to historical changes in the structure of socialization conditions.* The importance of the family has often been overestimated in comparison with other socialization contexts, especially organized educational establishments such as preschools and schools, but also in comparison with peer groups and groups of friends. The family takes a dominant role in the socialization process only during the first 10 years of childhood. In this period, it functions as the central reference group and can also exert a strong influence on the forms of care and education outside the family. By the beginning of schooling, at the latest, a slow detachment of the children from the family occurs, which is accelerated by the changeover to secondary school. In addition to organizations for child care and education, other organized societal subsystems increasingly become reference systems, including the mass media. At the same time, the status of the peer group increases considerably (Youniss, 1980; Clausen, 1986b, p. 72).

During the first 10 years of the child's life, the family retains its function as the child's central social point of reference and social mediator for the processing of external reality. Early adolescence brings a marked reduction in the family's direct influence on the children's life-style. Adolescents spend a lot of time outside the familial community. In particular, peer groups, with their opportunities for equal participation and the possibility of experiencing independence, have a great attraction and exert much influence on the development of personality. As studies of adolescence have shown, the temporal intensity of the adolescents' membership in such peer groups has grown markedly in the last 30 years. Relationships to partners of the opposite sex also begin earlier and are more intensive than they were a generation ago (Hurrelmann, Rosewitz, and Wolf, 1985, p. 70).

It is important to estimate correctly the significance of peer groups in the process of socialization. They particularly allow possibilities of self-development and self-realization in the area of emotional and sexual contacts and in the area of leisure time and consumer behavior, and they permit the experience of social recognition, security, and solidarity outside the educationally defined relationships in the family and school. However, it is clear that in normal cases the family retains its influence on the shape of adolescents' life in the areas of basic normative and ethical orientations and future planning for school and profession (Biddle, Bank, and Marlin, 1980). Over and above this, even after adolescents have left home the family, as a rule, remains an important social, and in some areas also emotional, reference and orientation point.

Future research must make allowances for the changed status of the family in the socialization process by analyzing more carefully than before the complementary and competitive relationships between the family and the other socialization contexts. Previous studies have made it clear that the increasing influence of kindergartens, other preschool establishments, schools, peer groups, media, and leisure activities does involve a relative reduction in familial influences and their shift to a few, though central, dimensions of childrens' and adolescents' personality development and to economic, social, cultural, and emotional background functions. For a better understanding of the changing importance of familial socialization, more longitudinal and historically comparative studies of the type that have been initiated by Elder (1974, 1979, 1985) are necessary. In these studies, the continual interchange between families and other institutional contexts is documented by analyzing the impact of historical change on the life cycle of the family, as well as on the life course of its individual members.

Another important area of historically oriented studies is the comparison of educational values. Because of the historically changed working and living conditions and the consolidation of welfare state safeguards, many class-specific contours of social and material living conditions that were still very clearly defined in the 1950s in all industrialized countries can be seen to have broken down during the last three decades. This change is evidently accompanied by a breakdown in the contrasts in the general value orientations and ideas on education among different population groups. A historical comparison of the research findings of socialization studies shows that in all families, value orientations that are directed at strict regulation of childhood behavior have weakened. It is evident that this reflects a change in general societal value orientations and social forms of interaction that is the result not only of socioeconomic but also historicocultural changes.

Social structure and personality development

Hierarchically structured and authoritarian forms of behavior between parents and children, and between educators and students, have declined. It is, however, worth asking whether the educators' dismantling of external pressures does not mean an increase in repressive psychological pressures and whether the use of power, influence, and even force has not simply retreated into the microstructures of interaction and communication. The high prevalence of child neglect, abuse, and maltreatment points in this direction. The investigation of these relations is an important assignment for future research (Garbarino, Schellenbach, and Sebes, 1986).

Summary

Past research on the role of the family in socialization has suffered from serious methodological and theoretical deficits that future research must seek to remedy. Nevertheless, research to date has also resulted in important findings, which can be summarized as follows.

1. *The social and material environment that the members of a family confront functions as a framing condition for the child's process of education and socialization.* Both macrostructural studies on work experiences and microstructural investigations of the internal social world of the family arrive at the finding that one can differentiate among familial socialization processes that vary according to social living conditions.

2. *In all recent investigative approaches, the family is understood as an interaction system of persons who productively process reality.* The personal experiences of a member of the family at his or her place of work or other areas outside the family do not transfer to the interaction and communication among the members of the family in a mechanical and linear manner. Even if we know the personality features and value orientations of all the members of a family, this is not sufficient to tell us the structure of interaction and communication that is characteristic for that family. This structure cannot be explained by adding together personality features and individual value orientations but only through investigating the reciprocal interactions among these features, in correspondence with the respective patterns of living conditions.

3. *It can likewise be maintained that the structure of familial interaction and communication does not have mechanical repercussions on a child's personality structures. As an autonomous person, the child productively interacts with the given reality that is formed through the family.* An essential role in this is played by the specific constellation of a child's personality features, such as, for example, the temperament and vivacity that express themselves in certain forms of participation in the environment or the way of shaping social contacts. According to the given features of personality, particular stimuli and opportunities in the social environment are either accepted or rejected.

4. *Each family functions for its members as a dynamic and relatively autonomous mediator of external reality.* The degree of complexity of the structures within families fulfills an essential role in shaping the socialization process for all their members. Thus, a relatively undifferentiated interaction structure results in a less complex translation and transformation of conditions of external reality. The degree of complexity of inner-family interaction structures relates to the objectively identifiable social and material living conditions in which the members of the family are placed.

5. *Children from all social groups in the population are evidently prepared for those social, verbal, cognitive, and emotional competences that are necessary for life in their subcultural family world.* In the process of growing up, both the children and the other members of the family learn the competences that are suited for "social survival" in their subculture. Although the family is a relatively autonomous social unit that is not directly exposed to the influences of external society, living conditions function as powerful background forces for the interaction and communication events within the family.

6. *The most important antecedent factors for the process of socialization are subject to historical processes of change. These changes in the social contexts of socialization have particularly influenced the status of familial education and socialization.* This can be seen in the qualification of the influence of the family in comparison with other socialization authorities, such as organized educational establishments, informal groups of friends and peer groups, and the mass media of entertainment and communication. In the last two or three decades, they have become important fellow educa-

tors and socializers alongside the family, and their influence within the family system has to be considered.

OCCUPATIONAL AND ADULT SOCIALIZATION

What significance do the effects of familial socialization have on the preoccupational and occupational careers of its young members? The preceding analysis of the conditions and structures of familial socialization clearly showed that the central function of the family remains, as in the past, to prepare its children for those social and cognitive competences that are necessary for everyday life in the respective subcultural social world. Depending on the conditions of the life situation, variously differentiated and complex abilities and skills for coping with life tasks and social demands in fields outside of the family are conveyed in the process of familial interaction and communication. The family's own resources of competence prove to be very important in meeting the demands for performance at school, vocational training, and work.

Educational career and social status attainment

It is within the schools that an individual's achievements are measured, evaluated, and ranked relative to others, according to fixed, formal criteria – criteria that later lead to the awarding of school-leaving certificates in some countries, or diplomas. An essential preselection for social position in the occupational system is linked to the type of school-leaving certificate.

A central theme of socialization research, which has become increasingly important in recent years because of its consequences for the life course, is the investigation of the origins and consequences of success and failure in school. School difficulties must be understood as the result of an insufficient fit between preconditions of learning that are specific to the life situation of an individual and the institutional learning requirements of the school. The individual's coping with the school's social and cognitive demands in these cases does not develop in the way that the school requires when measured against the school norms. The institutional requirements regarding social, motivational, emotional, cognitive, and verbal competences do not agree with the abilities of the student that have essentially been acquired in the familial socialization (Woods and Hammersley, 1977).

During the time spent at school, there generally occurs a pre-programming of the social career that strongly influences the position of a young member of society as an adult (Sewell and Hauser, 1975). Statistics show how unequally these positions are distributed: Children from different social strata do not receive a share of the various educational careers proportionate to their numbers in the total population (Persell, 1977, p. 135; Collins, 1979, p. 35). From their very first day at school, children from high-status families achieve better than the rest, and this privileged position continues with increasing strength throughout attendance at school. It is evident that children from low-status families are, on average, less able to fulfill the specific cognitive and social expectations and requirements.

The very tense situation in the job market since the 1970s has noticeably increased the importance of high school leaving grades. They are a necessary – though not always sufficient – prerequisite for access to attractive vocational training and professional positions (Hurrelmann, 1987). Both low- and high-status families attempt to retain or improve their positions through increased school training for their children: Children from middle- and upper-class families must develop strategies that will avoid a drop in social status and lead to a career that is typical for their class. Children from the lower social classes have to develop strategies that, despite the increased competition, will grant them the most favorable starting position for the transition to vocational life (Collins, 1979, p. 191).

Particularly in Europe, efforts to optimize the chances for a smooth transition from school to work can be found in the behavioral strategies of adolescents from all social classes. In order to retain the same social status, present-day students must achieve educational qualifications that are at least one formal stage of qualification higher than those of their parents' generation. Thus, for example, children from working-class families in West Germany are obliged to attend school at least two years longer than their parents did, since they fear that the old eight-year course will not provide access to a vocational activity that will meet the social aspirations of their parents. Children from the upper social strata must strive for the best school-leaving grades possible in order to gain admittance to university (which has become increasingly difficult, because of higher entrance requirements in several courses of study), or at least to secure a high-level occupational position after school. All school leavers are forced to adopt specific strategies in order to optimize their vocational starting positions (Hurrelmann, 1984).

Thus, in modern industrialized societies the competition between the social classes for the best starting positions in the work market takes place mostly at school. It is a competition with unequal starting positions, because, as has been shown, children from the middle and upper classes are much better able to adopt and maintain optimization strategies, since they can better adjust to the rules of the school system. These families protect their privileged position by no longer just making economic investments in the traditional manner but by increasingly investing "cultural capital": They make sure that their children achieve the necessary educational qualifications that will secure the family's status (DiMaggio, 1982; Bourdieu, 1984, p. 255).

Structural analyses of participation in education demonstrate the effects of this process very clearly: In Europe, although school attendance of 16- to 18-year-olds has risen greatly within the last three decades, the composition of this group according to social classes has scarcely changed. Bourdieu (1984) has shown that in France there has been no shift in the structure of the relations of school attendance among the classes as a consequence of the expansion of the educational system. Instead it appears that the various changes have had the effect of canceling each other out. As Bourdieu's analysis shows, children from those social strata that have relied for many generations on economic reproduction mechanisms – factory owners, employers, and farmers – have greatly increased their participation in education over the last 20 years and have thus secured their status through cultural reproduction mechanisms. Despite the increased participation in education that, at the same time, can be seen among working-class families, these retain a lower-rank position, whereas the independent professionals, high-status managerial and technical workers, officials, and other members of the upper middle classes have maintained their already superior positions through increased effort. These studies make it very clear how strongly the social and material living conditions of a family form the starting point for the shaping of the educational and the occupational career, even under historically changing conditions.

In order to analyze the importance of the school years for the individual life course, and particularly for the occupational career, we investigated 14- to 21-year-old West German adolescents' estimates and evaluations of their educational and occupational aspirations and achievements over a period of seven years (Hurrelmann, 1988). Because of the longitudinal nature of the study, it was possible to record both the prospective and retrospective views and evaluations of the adolescents. The study shows that the changes in the conditions of learning and work at school and their increased accent on competition are sensitively perceived by the adolescents. They see school as a biographically most important time in their own lives that will have a strong determining influence on their occupational career.

As our study shows, the majority of adolescents, whether successful or unsuccessful at school, interpret their educational careers as being instrumental: Training in school is given the status of "means of gaining certificates." They indicate that school has a very high status for the shaping of their future in its formal determination, without at the same time according it significance as an orientational help and support in meeting the concrete demands of life in the present. As a consequence, the students who do badly and leave school with poor qualifications regard their school years as a rather unprofitable phase of their lives. For them, this is a part of life that is wasted, since it provides no directly evaluable advantages that will influence their subsequent occupational careers. But even successful students have great difficulty in finding any immediate value for their own lives in their experience at school. They suffer from the awareness that their time at school is dictated by the securing of status and the optimization of possibilities (Hurrelmann, Engel, Holler, and Nordlohne, 1988). Schools must become more aware of their biographical importance to adolescents and adapt to the consequences of the historically changed situation and the adolescents' subjective interpretation of the school years as part of the life course.

Social structure and personality development

Occupational socialization

The role of student has a comparatively low status in society. It is the embodiment of incompleteness and an externally visible indicator of not being adult. This marginal position in society stands in sharp contrast to the high individual and biographical significance that is accorded to the achievement record at school, which is documented by school reports and (in Europe) by leaving certificates. This situation changes rapidly once the transition to an occupational status is completed. As soon as vocational activity starts, the publicly ascribed social importance and the individually and biographically experienced significance come together. If we follow the pattern of interpretation that the students in our study used, preparation for life is now at an end, and "real life" begins (Hurrelmann, 1987).

The start of vocational training symbolizes the first and most decisive step in leaving adolescence and entering adulthood. The transition from school to work is a change from an educational to a work organization. From a social-ecological perspective, this transition for adolescents usually results in a change in their social network, an alteration in the daily schedule, and an introduction to the mechanism of material payment for gainful employment. Consequently, the interaction with the demand structures of vocational training and gainful employment can cause crucial changes in features of personality, action competences, and self-concepts.

During vocational training, adolescents have to make realistic estimates of their possibilities for vocational development and their future career perspectives, and they must correct or qualify their earlier goals. The ideas developed at school now have to be brought into line with the actual possibilities ahead. A process of cooling off high-flying plans and desires occurs. As vocational training continues, it becomes increasingly harder to change a course that has once been chosen and to carry out any extensive modifications to the occupational career. As empirical studies show, potential discontents and desires for change are increasingly repressed by the adolescents. This is joined by the adolescents' realization that a long-term career perspective can unfold only with great uncertainty (Grasso and Shea, 1979; Heinz, 1980).

Nevertheless, starting to work and beginning a vocational career are considered to be the social backbone of adult existence, even under changing conditions such as the significant reduction in the length of the working day and the accompanying growth in leisure time (Clausen, 1981). Occupational activity is a basic guarantee of material independence and an essential symbol of social autonomy as a citizen.

This career effect is not the only crucial factor for occupational socialization; also important are the structuring effects of the types of vocational activity that were mentioned earlier in this chapter, namely the degree of independence, the nature of the work, and the position within a work hierarchy. The organizational climate of a workplace, with its particular structuring of technical, interactive, and communicative aspects, develops a socialization environment that has a lasting effect throughout the individual's entire working career.

One of the main goals of research in this field is to analyze how individual abilities and competences are connected with specific economic and technical demands and lead to development of the qualifications that are required in the working process. Analyses of this type can help to assess how occupational socialization, when compared with preoccupational and extraoccupational socialization, affects the formation and development of personality.

From the perspective of socialization theory, the relations between preoccupational, occupational, and extraoccupational areas of influence are of great interest in determining the status of vocational work in the shaping of the life history. As has been said, it is evident that working conditions have a strong effect on features of personality and on life-style (Kohn and Schooler, 1983). But inversely, the familial context, social living conditions, the type and quality of education, and the individual biographical conceptions affect the form and way in which working conditions are experienced and possibly changed. For example, the ideas and perspectives on vocational work that are present in the family, which are strongly influenced by the occupational career and the concrete working conditions of the parents, prove to be particularly significant for the forms of coping with work demands that are shown by the children (Heinz, 1980, p. 517).

Adult socialization

In the last two decades, socialization research has paid increasing attention to the conditions and processes of personality development that occur after childhood, adolescence, and early adulthood with the beginning of employment. In this area, recent research has complied with the propositions formulated in chapter 2 that define socialization as a lifelong process of interacting with the social and material environment. The initial impetus came from rapid technological change and the accompanying need for vocational reeducation, further education, and more training on the job. Processes of development and change in adult personality are frequently addressed with particular attention to far-reaching changes in the family cycle (e.g., changes in the family constellation through the children's leaving home or the death of one of the parents) and in the vocational field (e.g., changes in working conditions and life-style through upward or downward social mobility, change of job, unemployment, or retirement) (Hurrelmann, 1986).

Because of these impulses, socialization theory finds itself on the path toward a theory of lifelong personality development, with a theoretical orientation toward the entire span of life (Clausen, 1986b; Sorensen, Weinert, and Sherrod, 1986). The individual phases of life across the entire life span are understood as part of a temporal sequence, and an analysis is made of the effects that continuities and discontinuities in this sequence have on the person. The individual life history is conceived of a socially regulated movement of the person through the age and social structure of the society, in which every transition into a new configuration of living conditions places new demands on individual competences and self-concept (Eichhorn, Clausen, Haan, Honzik, and Mussen, 1984; Neugarten and Hagestad, 1985; Riley, 1985; Mayer and Müller, 1986).

From this perspective, life presents numerous transitions that are linked to social roles associated with age, law, or custom: for example, the transition from infancy to childhood, from childhood to adolescence, from adolescence to adult status, from the early to the later phase of adulthood, retirement from work, and preparation for death (Rosenmayr, 1978; Runyan, 1978; Bush and Simmons, 1981; Clausen, 1986a). The types of demands on action competences and self-concept with which the individual is faced at every transition are comparable, but the decisive qualitative difference between the early transitions in the life history and the later, subsequent ones can be seen to be that with the beginning of adulthood the personality no longer finds itself in a process of construction and formation but in a process of modifying already existing structures and continuing to develop them.

Every transition requires reorganizations and redefinitions of the self-image that are mostly linked to attaining a balance between earlier experiences and events and anticipations of future experiences and events (Kohli, 1980, p. 311). Many indicators support the idea that it is not only at the end of the adolescent phase but also at the end of the early adult phase that particularly far-reaching crises of personal reorganization occur. In both cases, it is not just biological and physiological changes that are decisive for this (in the first case sexual maturity, and in the second the arrival at the peak of physical power and the beginning of decline) but also socially defined actualities. In the crisis of adolescence, it is the assertion of independence from the parents and the securing through school and vocation of future social status that are decisive, whereas the midlife crisis involves a recognition of the discrepancy between earlier standards, goals, and desires in the vocational and biographical field and realizing those demands that are still realistically possible (Clausen, 1981, 1986b, p. 162).

Midlife crisis terminates the era of early adulthood with a review and reappraisal of what has been done to date. Alongside those who have not realized their aspirations we can find those who have achieved their goals or who are still upwardly mobile. Most men and women in their forties have made a realistic assessment of their future chances for investments in career and personal life. But some recognize that the goals that they have achieved do not provide them with the satisfaction and wish fulfillment that they had hoped for. The desires and aspirations for one's own biography that are developed during adolescence are, to a certain extent, refreshed and reactivated in midlife. They become a conscious component of the history of the individual and the self-image with which one has to cope or come to terms with under conditions of personal life that are now very hard to change.

Social structure and personality development

When we consider the predominant social pattern of interpretation of our achievement-oriented society ("Everybody has the same opportunities to start with – everybody makes their own decisions about their occupational and social position in life through their individual achievements"), we can see that the midlife balancing process can become a serious stressor if material and social living conditions fall below those of societally comparable reference groups or earlier personal aspirations. This constellation can intensify if the children of the family, whose process of detachment generally occurs in the middle of the parents' life, have also not attained the starting position in school and occupation desired by the parents.

Within socialization theory, there are strongly divergent views of the relative importance of the individual phases of life. The extreme alternatives are (1) absolute dominance of the early phases of life, and (2) equal importance of all phases of life (cf. Kohli, 1986). Both alternatives are hard to prove empirically. The idea of the primacy of the earlier phases of life remains to this day the most widespread. In psychoanalysis and the early functional theories, in particular, childhood is regarded as the most important phase in the socialization process (Freud, 1949; Parsons and Bales, 1955). Influences in later phases of life are regarded as negligible or of little importance. The latter view is, for example, expressed in the conceptual differentiation of "primary" and "secondary" socialization. In contrast, learning theory, ecological and developmental psychology, as well as action theory, have stressed that this conception goes astray when the significance of adulthood is considered. For example, research in learning psychology has shown that, given sufficient stimulation in the social environment, the ability and willingness to learn is retained well into old age (even if some conditions – for example, speed and short-term memory – deteriorate) (cf. Baltes and Brim, 1979). Intraindividual variability is not restricted to one phase of life but is spread across the entire life span (Clausen, 1986b, p. 142).

It is hard to establish the absolute dominance of any single phase of life. Therefore, for future theory and research we need more differentiated concepts that assume a subsequent sedimentation and layering of individual experiences, biographically relevant self-concepts, and social competences from one phase in the life course to the next. Although changed constellations of living, working, and learning are taken in and processed in a way that is specific to each situation, each individual has to refer back to the repertoire of forms and the patterns of action and behavior that have proved themselves in previous situations. In general, earlier experiences have a special weight because of this, but they can be overlapped and covered over by later experiences, so that their significance for the development of personality is qualified (Clausen, 1986b).

How great the weight of early socialization is, and to what extent the personality can still change in adulthood, are interesting and decisive questions that must be answered by future research in the field of adult socialization. We need to clarify, in detail, for which dimensions of personality formation and development the earlier phases of the biography are more important than the later ones, and how the experiences and events overlap one another. There are probably differences in the forms of acquisition and processing of external and internal reality among the individual life phases, and the way they interrelate requires precise investigation. For example, comparative longitudinal studies show that there is a compensatory effect in the life course whereby deficiencies in socialization in early phases of life are (under certain circumstances) balanced out in later phases, and vice versa (Elder, 1979, 1981).

Research in this area has to rely heavily on interdisciplinary approaches that focus on both the biological and the sociocultural character of human development. Obviously, during the process of aging the biogenetic vital potentials within the cellular, tissue, and organ systems decrease, and the individual's ability to adapt to environmental variations is therefore reduced, especially in stressful situations. On the level of cellular and dendrite brain functioning, however, growth and deterioration occur concomitantly at all stages of life, including old age. That is, biological aging and intellectual aging are relatively independent of one another. Individual life-style, training, and activities, on the one hand, and social and material living conditions on the other play a role as moderating variables. As with any other phase of life, it is important for old age that we take into account the interplay among biological, psychological, and cultural potentials and constraints (Baltes, Dittmann-Kohli, and Dixon, 1986).

4

SUCCESSFUL
AND UNSUCCESSFUL
SOCIALIZATION

W HAT are the preconditions for successful or unsuccessful
socialization? What conditions must be present in order to
ensure a satisfactory development of personality that will fit both
individual and societal criteria? We will explore these questions in
this final chapter by taking a closer look at three of the propositions for a comprehensive approach to socialization that were formulated in chapter 2. The essence of propositions 6, 7, and 8 can
be summarized as follows:

- *Proposition 6:* The competence for interactive and communicative
  action is a prerequisite for a person's ability to manage the
  demands and requirements of everyday situations in the span of
  the life course. Competence for action can be effective only if it
  takes into account and deals with a person's own motives, needs,
  and interests.
- *Proposition 7:* In order to process and manage external and internal reality effectively, a person needs a reflected self-image and
  identity. "Identity" means continuity of self-experience on the
  basis of the self-concept. As we have already noted, under present
  conditions the formation and maintenance of a continuity of self-
  experience is more difficult than it was one or two generations
  ago, because social roles and situations are more subject to rapid
  change.
- *Proposition 8:* Whether or not socialization is successful is decided
  according to how suitable a person's action competences, self-
  concept, and identity formation are for the developmental tasks.
  If the structure and profile of the behavioral repertoire are not
  sufficiently developed, there is a risk that psychological and
  socially deviant forms of behavior will arise that may interfere
  with further development of the personality.

This chapter examines each of these three propositions in turn.
First we will consider the construction of the action competences

and self-concept that are the basis for the formation of identity as a biographical experience of continuity. In the second section we will investigate the consequences for individual behavior and action that result from an inadequate development of action competences. Some of the ways in which problem behavior and deviant behavior emerge and manifest are discussed. The third section of the chapter is concerned with preventive and corrective interventions in the socialization process that are intended either to prevent disorders in personality development or to remove disorders that have already developed. It is proposed that the goal of all social, educational, and psychological interventions that are derived from socialization theory should be (1) to place a person in a position in which he or she can cope with the demands of situations in such a way that they provide potiential for the further development of his or her personality, and (2) to shape social environments that are capable of stimulating and supporting successful personality development.

THE DEVELOPMENT OF ACTION COMPETENCE AND IDENTITY

In chapter 2, I used the term "processing of external and internal reality" to describe the acquisition of and confrontation between social and material/natural living conditions and personal needs and motives. The social and material environment is perceived by the senses; then sorted, evaluated, and interpreted according to social values and norms; and finally balanced with personal needs and emotions and personal plans. The execution of this processing requires certain basic abilities and skills in sensory, motor, affective, cognitive, and interactive areas. Each single procedure of confrontation with inner and outer reality simultaneously changes these skills and abilities and develops them further. The concept of processing also means a "working on oneself," in which impressions and experiences have to be brought into accord with the previous states of comprehension, experiences, and observations.

Preconditions for the formation of action competence

Each individual endeavors to unfold the powers and abilities that are contained within him- or herself and to bring them under personal control. In the course of productively processing reality, one's personal abilities and skills are discovered, developed, further developed, and consolidated. In the course of personality development, a progressive mastery of these abilities and skills is achieved that permits an increasingly differentiated reception and observation of one's personal needs, more suitable ways of adapting to living conditions, and, at the same time, the development of an increasing ability to shape and master external reality. This process of acquiring and confronting external and internal reality continues throughout life but has particularly prominent phases during childhood and adolescence.

The abilities and skills that are preconditions for social action can be understood only by analyzing the process of interaction between persons that is carried out through reciprocal interpretations of social situations. The exchange of definitions of situations occurs only if the partners in interactions are both able and willing to place themselves reciprocally in the social position of the other and accept this role-taking perspective as the starting point for their own action. The result of social exchange and communication can be understood to be the construction of complex abilities and skills that suitably guide personal behavior in different situations in accordance with personal interests and needs. Action is the intentional and active realization of goals that are the product of the perception of the situation, the goal orientation, and the conception of the means for achieving these goals.

"Action competence" can be described as *the state of the individual availability and suitable application of abilities and skills for interacting with the social and material environment.* It can be understood as the state of the individual availability of strategies of behavior, interaction, and communication that allow a suitable activity in concrete social situations and a coordination of the demands of the various situations that are of significance for the person and/or the environment, including emotions and affective demands.

The basis and precondition for the formation of action competences is the development of those basic abilities and skills that permit a person to perceive the social and material environment and to interact with it, using all of the senses. These basic competences include sensory, motor, interactive, intellectual, and affective abilities and skills:

- Sensory (e.g., the ability to smell and to see)
- Motor (e.g., the ability to move one's limbs)
- Interactive (e.g., the ability to take over the role of another person)
- Intellectual (e.g., the ability to process information; capacity for storing knowledge)
- Affective (e.g., the ability to monitor one's emotions; emotional commitment to others; empathy)

Such fundamental abilities generally develop during the first years of life. They are based on the very earliest experiences in which the child builds up a relationship of trust and deep affective bonding with the parents or guardians (Brim and Kagan, 1980, Flavell and Ross, 1981). This process of the development of basic skills and abilities is just as much encouraged by maturation processes within the organism as by stimulus from the social and material environment, and it leads to the formation of action competences. As soon as the structural features of the sensory, motor, interactive, intellectual, and affective abilities and skills have reached such a high state of differentiation and complexity, and such a high degree of reflectivity, that they permit a self-monitoring and independent interaction and communication, we can talk about action competences. The development of abilities and skills is the basis for the unfolding of competences. In a number of qualitative leaps that occur during childhood and adolescence, competences develop out of the abilities and skills in the various fields just listed through differentiation, growth in complexity, and an increase in reflectivity (Doise and Palmonari, 1984).

For heuristic purposes, it is helpful to categorize competences according to different dimensions of action. We can differentiate among cognitive, moral, emotional, verbal, social, and aesthetic competences, each of which describes the availability and the application of abilities and skills in specific, analytically separable dimensions and fields of a person's activities. Since the various dimensions are interlinked and mutually influence one another, however, this differentiation is justified only for the sake of analysis. When combined, these abilities and skills form the operative

107

basis for a person's social and instrumental activity, in the sense of a productive processing of reality.

The interrelations among the individual dimensions of competence offer a fundamental constellation for social and instrumental action that, though internally structured, is continually open to change. This constellation can be defined as the *structure of the action competence* of an individual. This structure of action competence describes the specific relation of the cognitive, moral, aesthetic, emotional, verbal, and social dimensions of competence – for example, the potential for the perception of the environment; the guidance of action according to ethical and moral principles; the emotional opening up of the social and natural environment; the verbal naming and encoding of external reality; the ability to make social contact; and the confidence in behavior – that are available and applicable at a specific point of time during the life of the individual.

Action competence, developmental tasks, and living conditions

In everyday life and throughout life, each person is exposed to an endless multitude of different social situations in which he or she must be able to act by applying his or her competence. The respective individual structuring of action competence functions as a guiding authority for action and behavior in various situations. During the life course, there is a continual confrontation with new situations, each of which has to be mastered through the use of suitable action competence. Each person is continually confronted anew with the task of producing suitable relations with the social and material environment and adjusting his or her competence to altered situations.

Situational demands and possibilities basically differ according to their specific configurations during certain phases of life. The concept of a "developmental task" can be used to define *the specific pattern of behavioral demands that is characteristic for a specific phase of life* (Havighurst, 1972). By using this concept, it is possible to define specific structurings and configurations of action competences for the phases of childhood, adolescence, early adulthood, mature adulthood, and old age that are necessary for the mastering of situative actualities. We can identify different culturally and socially preordained expectations and demands for each phase of life. To some extent, they function as reference systems within which the structures of action competence have to develop.

For the adolescent phase of human life in modern industrialized societies, for example, we can classify the following developmental tasks (Hurrelmann, Rosewitz, and Wolf, 1985, p. 12):

- The development of an intellectual and social competence for independently acquiring scholastic and, subsequently, vocational qualifications, with the goal of taking up gainful employment and thereby securing the economic and material basis for an autonomous existence as an adult.
- The development of the gender role and a heterosexual relationship with a partner that can provide a long-term basis for raising children and building up one's own family.
- The development of a personal value and norm system, and an ethical and political consciousness, that are in agreement with personal behavior and action, permitting, over the long term, responsible action in this field.
- The development of personal patterns of behavior for exploiting the consumer goods and leisure time markets, with the goal of developing a personal life-style and arriving at an autonomously shaped and need-oriented interaction with the corresponding opportunities.

It is clear that these developmental tasks differ qualitatively from those of childhood. Childhood is mainly involved with the development of basic sensory, motor, interactive, intellectual, and affective abilities that are on a lower level of development from those of adolescense. This distinguishes those developmental tasks that are typical for childhood from those that are typical for adolescence (Newman and Newman, 1975). Similar statements can be made about the demarcation between adolescence and adulthood: The transition to adulthood is possible only if all of the developmental tasks that have been mentioned as being typical for adolescence have been mastered.

The mastering of the behavioral demands in the various fields of action that are characteristic for a specific phase of life is possible only if a suitable structure of cognitive, moral, emotional, verbal, and social competences is formed. It is important to remember that it is not just necessary to construct suitable action competences for the individual fields of activity (achievement, partner relations, politics, leisure, and so forth), but, at the same time, it is also necessary to coordinate the various demands from the different fields.

The coordination of different behavioral demands requires (1) the setting up of a highly differentiated, very complex, and, at the same time reflectively guided structuring of competences for coping with situative demands, and (2) the ability to compromise between the various demands and the expectations of other persons, on the one hand, and short- or long-term personal needs, desires, and goal orientations on the other. The available action competences must be composed in such a way that they permit the satisfaction of situative demands and, at the same time, allow for personal needs. This requires a certain inner distance from these demands, and virtuosity and creativity in the organization of personal actions.

Concepts from interaction theory describe these specific features of competence as "role distance" and "tolerance of ambiguity" (Goffman, 1972). The more flexible these strategies, and the stronger their reflectivity – that is, their availability to the individual's perception, observation, and appraisal – the more favorable are the preconditions for adequate behavior, because the objectively present degrees of freedom of action in different situations can be exploited and external demands do not run into insoluble contradictions with internal needs.

The level of role distance and tolerance of ambiguity that are attained, as well as the quality of a person's action competence, are decisively influenced by the quality of the socialization context. This also implies that the availability of mechanisms and strategies for the productive processing of external and internal reality, and the possibilities for unfolding one's own personality, are in no way purely psychologically but also socially regulated. This is also true for the formation of the self-concept.

Action competence and self-concept

Proposition 7 asserts that the individual cannot become a subject who is capable of action without the construction of a self-concept. Such an image of oneself is an inner concept of the entirety of motives, attributes, attitudes, and action competences, as well as their cognitive evaluation and emotional appraisal, that a person gains when looking at his or her activities. The self-concept is formed through the conscious and unconscious processing of self-related information about the cognitive, moral, emotional, verbal, social, and aesthetic dimensions of the individual competences, information that is gained from the perception of personal activities during the process of confrontation with the social and material environment and with personal needs and interests.

The basis for the development of a self-concept is the ability to differentiate between oneself as a person and the surrounding reality. This basic ability has usually been developed by the end of the first year of life and is particularly expressed by, first, the visual recognition of one's own physical appearance and, second, the perception of oneself as socially differing from other persons (Goffman, 1972). It is evident that during childhood the various dimensions of the self-concept are only loosely connected to one another. As the personality develops, they are brought closer together, at the same time become more differentiated and comprehensive, and unite to form a structure in which there is either more or less agreement. The ideas and presumptions about oneself as a person that already exist influence and then guide the reception of new information about the self. The more differentiated the perceptions, appraisals, and evaluations of the information one has about onself, the more realistic is the self-concept, and the more appropriate are the impulses for personal behavior and further development of personality (Hausser, 1983, p. 32).

As Rosenberg's work has shown, social factors play a major role in the formation of the self-concept:

> The self-concept is not present at birth but arises out of social experience and interaction; it both incorporates and is influenced by the individual's location in the social structure; it is formed within institutional systems, such as the family, school, economy, church; it is constructed from the materials of the culture; and it is affected by immediate social and environmental contexts. In other words, the self-concept achieves its particular shape and form in the matrix of a given culture, social structure and institutional system. Although the individual's view of himself may be internal, what he sees and feels when the thinks of himself is largely the product of social life. (Rosenberg, 1981, p. 593)

The self-concept is not just composed of the results of self-perception but is also a product of self-appraisal. The self-concept reflects one's individual opinion about the properties, attributes, and features of oneself as a person and also reflects one's individual abilities and skills in mastering developmental tasks, and it always necessarily contains strong emotional components (Weinstein, 1969). The emotional tone of the picture one has of oneself is all the more important when we consider that, as with all attitudes, attitudes toward the self are normally transferred from one area to the next, and from one point in time to the next, so that such attitudes are subject to a process of generalization. Attitudes toward oneself in areas that are central to the self-concept can have such a generalizing significance for the self-concept in its entirety. The more central such an area, the larger its emotional strength. Thus, self-appraisal with a positive emotional tone is a necessary precondition for a healthy development of personality. Negative emotional tones generally indicate uncertainty and instability in the process of self-evaluation. This is not to imply that one should overlook the less positive sides of oneself as a person when compiling the self-concept but only that the positive elements should predominate when all areas of the self-image are balanced out.

In present-day societies, the areas of achievement in education and occupation, instrumental problem solving, and interindividual social relations must be considered to be among the central areas from which information is transferred to the self-concept. For this reason, the partial self-images of general achievement ability, problem solving, sociability, and attractiveness have to be given the most important position among the instruments for assessing the general self-image (Weinstein, 1969; Rosenberg, 1981, p. 608).

The establishing of a self-concept is possible only because of the unique human capacity for self-objectification, that is, serving as the object of one's own observation and action. This capacity was first stressed in the work of Mead (1934, p. 138) and was later elaborated by Rosenberg, among others:

> Not only is the human capable of conceiving of himself, but he is also capable of behavioral interpretation (reflecting on and interpreting one's own behavior), introspection (inspecting one's inner thoughts and feelings), self-regulation (treating the self as an object or instrument of one's purposes), verbal interpretation (responding to one's own verbal expressions), self-reinforcement (punishing

or rewarding the self), self-presentation (setting forth a certain self in interaction), and others. (Rosenberg, 1981, p. 623)

The capacities for self-objectification and self-regulation, which provide feedback on personal action and the impulses that alter and extend action competence, can be developed only in face-to-face interaction and within social and cultural contexts. In the process of interaction and communication, each person has to take the role of the other and see the world, including him- or herself, from the other's perspective. The attitudes of our significant interaction partners provide highly relevant feedback for shaping our self-concepts. Our self-concepts correspond, at least partially, to the views of us held by other people whose judgements we trust and value:

> The individual experiences himself as such, not directly, but only indirectly, from the particular standpoints of other individual members of the same social group, or from the generalized standpoint of the social group as a whole to which he belongs. For he enters his own experience as a self or individual, not directly or immediately, not by becoming a subject to himself, but only insofar as he first becomes an object to himself just as other individuals are objects to him or in his experience; and he becomes an object to himself only by taking the attitudes of other individuals toward himself within a social environment or context of experience and behavior in which both he and they are involved. (Mead, 1934, p. 138)

There is some evidence to suggest that in the interest of positive self-appraisals and self-esteem, as well as in the interest of establishing consistency of information concerning oneself, each person engages in selective perception of the attitudes of others and in selective attribution of significance. The result of this interpersonal selectivity is that we attribute greater significance to the opinions of those whose attitudes toward us are more favorable (Rosenberg, 1981, p. 601). For accurate and appropriate feedback on personal actions, however, each person has to rely on self-related information that is as realistic and comprehensive as possible and does not favor structurally distorted patterns of the processing of reality.

Social structure and personality development

Self-concept and identity

The self-concept, as the structured framework of the results of self-perception and self-appraisal, is the necessary source of the individual state called "identity." When we speak of "identity," we mean that a person retains a continuity of self-experience across different social roles and different biographical phases that is based on the self-concept. The continuity of self-experience – in other words, the experience of oneself as always being the same – not only relates to the different stages of the personal biography but also to the various behavioral demands from different fields and areas of activity (social roles) in which a person operates within each respective phase of life.

The concept of identity has several origins in scientific discussion. In psychoanalytic theory, the concept developed by Erikson (1959) has gained widespread acceptance. According to Erikson, the main precondition for the consolidation of personality is a progression through various psychosocial crises in childhood and adolescence: Each state of human development is marked by a crucial issue for the self-experience in its relation to the external and internal world. In infancy, there is a tension between trust and mistrust; in childhood between initiative to gain more autonomy and guilt if this initiative is prohibited; in adolescence, the fundamental developmental crisis lies in overcoming the tension between identity and role confusion. At the end of adolescence, there occurs a relatively stable integration of inner needs and outer demands. For Erikson, identity is the synthesis of the experiences of passing through sequential developmental stages. The feeling of identity is the accumulated confidence that the unity and continuity that is observed by others corresponds to an ability to retain an internal unity and continuity.

In sociological theory, some dimensions of the concept of the self as it has been developed by Mead (1934, p. 135) have been picked up and expanded by, among others, Goffman (1963, 1972), Krappmann (1969), and Rosenberg and Gara (1985). They understand identity as a balancing process that has to deal with changing situative demands, on the one hand, and changing life experiences on the other. Goffman (1963) describes the continuity and consistency of the self-experience of coping with the demands of various social roles and fields of action as the individual's "social identity." He uses the term "personal identity" to describe the continuity and consistency of the individual's self-experience in the course of changing biographical circumstances. In the case of the social identity, a person is expected to subordinate him- or herself to the general social norms that, in principle, are directed at all persons. In the case of personal identity, on the other hand, a person, because of his or her unique attributes and personality features, is expected to distinguish him- or herself from other persons. Thus, a person is simultaneously required to be "like everybody else" and to be "like nobody else" and has to find a balance on both dimensions. Habermas has also made a valuable contribution to identity theory, providing us with important insights concerning identity formation and maintenance (1976, p. 67). His theory specifies the societal and individual conditions that must be fulfilled if a person is to be able to sufficiently maintain his or her identity: On the side of society, flexible norm systems that leave room for subjective interpretation and an individual shaping of behavior; on the side of the individual, flexible and reflective capacities and competences for (inter-)action and communication.

All of the theoretical concepts mentioned agree in not regarding identity as a permanently successful and reliable possession of a person but rather as a state of self-experience that is continually subject to new processes of interpretation and negotiation with both the external environment and the personal inner nature. Identity must always be understood as a coordination process of the individual that includes confrontation with both external and internal reality. A person's structure of needs and interests, and also his or her action competences, do not have to agree with the respective institutionally and organizationally defined social expectations of the environment. The actual coordination achievement that is characteristic for the state called "identity" lies exactly in balancing and actively processing the tensions that, of necessity, arise from the lack of agreement between personal needs, social demands, and action competences.

More recent concepts of identity, within action theory and the theory of social structure, have not always paid sufficient attention to the emotional dimensions of identity formation. Because the primary interest has been in discovering the emancipatory conditions of social structure, analysis has concentrated on verbal and moral competences (Habermas, 1970). The relation of the person to external reality is often defined, one-sidedly, in terms of verbal processes, and sensory and emotional dimensions are neglected. However, actions must always be understood as being simultaneously verbal-reflective and sensory-impulsive, and this double nature must find expression in the concept of identity.

Identity and the life course

If we agree with Erikson's analysis of the psychodynamics involved (1959), we can assume that the individual capacities that are necessary for the construction of identity are not formed until adolescence. Accordingly, it is only after the completion of the adolescent phase that there is a sequence of psychosocial crises that have to be mastered in order to form the necessary structures of personality that lead to the development of identity. According to Erikson, the identity problem must be mastered at the end of adolescence, by a relatively conflict-free psychosocial compromise, if it is not to remain unresolved and fraught with conflict for the subsequent phases of life.

Erickson's view is supported by the fact that individual capacities for the development of identity are lacking in childhood, because of the incomplete development of action competences during this phase. The results of the processing of internal reality and its coordination with the results of the processing of external reality become increasingly available to consciousness during the adolescent phase. The relationship between a person's awareness of his or her existential living conditions, on the one side, and of his or her own body and its internal structure of needs, motivations, and interests on the other side, becomes increasingly more differentiated and complex and, during adolescence, achieves a stage of development that is qualitatively different from that of childhood. Increasing awareness of one's own personal needs and interests and their interrelations, combined with the ability to coordinate this awareness with personal competences in order to interact with external reality, depend on development, and it is only during adolescence that this achieves a qualitative stage that permits the construction of identity (Habermas, 1976, p. 94).

Thus, some arguments can be introduced that support the idea that it is only after adolescence that we can assume a certain quality in processing external and internal reality that has the necessary degree of self-awareness and reflectiveness to permit the experiencing of oneself as a person as being "identical with oneself." On the other hand, as has been mentioned earlier, the construction of a self-concept results from a synthesis of processes of self-perception and self-appraisal that already occurs during childhood. Also, the first approaches to an awareness of oneself as a person must be localized in childhood and certainly must leave traces of a continuity of self-experience. We can only ever deal with the analytic assessment of qualitative leaps in the development of self-experience, and we should not try to classify fixed categories for this process. This means that it is not possible to give an age-specific point of personality development at which time the capacities for the formation and maintenance of identity are given.

Moreover, it is highly evident that historical conditions for personality development during childhood and adolescence have changed during the last several decades. The major periods of the life course – the life phases of childhood, adolescence, young adulthood, adulthood, and old age – are formally differentiated from one another by socially, culturally, and legally defined demarcations. However, these demarcations are far from being effective for all spheres of everyday life. Thus, today, in the industrialized societies, fields of action are open to children and adolescents that were accessible only to adults a generation ago (Hurrelmann, Rosewitz, and Wolf, 1985, p. 59): for example, adolescents' drug consumption and the role of adolescents as consumers of goods and as an audience for the mass media. On the other hand, adults who experience long-term unemployment and/or who must reenter the systems of occupational and educational training can be robbed of an important identity-forming field of experience, namely gainful employment, that until a short time ago was regarded as a major constituent for the definition of the role of adulthood.

Changes in the economic structure of living conditions have evidently altered the context for identity formation in the various phases of life in such a way that the widespread idea of a definite completion of identity formation by the end of adolescence has to be regarded as problematic. It seems probable that until the 1940s, for the majority of the appropriate age groups a final determination of occupational decisions, with their consequences for the entire course of life, typically was linked to the end of adolescence, which was regarded then as occurring around the age of 18. This was a settling down to the most important social role of adulthood that was meant to possess a decisive power for the remainder of life.

The economically supported trajectories are no longer typical for the present adolescent generation. The transition to the adult-specific economic status follows differentiated tracks and is drawn out over a greater length of time than it was two or three generations ago. Through the postponement of the occupational career, the expansion of leisure time, widespread material wealth, and the availability of new life-styles in all phases of life, a greater individualization of important life decisions has become possible and necessary. At the same time, such decisions can be more easily and quickly altered than was the case 20 or 30 years ago.

Under present conditions, we have noted earlier, it appears that the formation and maintenance of a continuity of self-experience is more difficult than it was one or two generations ago. In modern societies age has become an important organizing and sequencing feature. We can observe a growing relevance of life stages and career sequences, and of chronological age as a criterion for their differentiation. The highly institutionalized life course provides reference points for personal orientation: It regulates the movement of individuals through their lives in terms of career pathways and age strata, and it regulates their biographically relevant actions of structuring their perspectives for movement through life (Kohli, 1986, p. 272). However, this sequencing of obligations and segregating of chances and opportunities (such as sequenced paths of education, rules concerning credentials for occupational transitions, and formalized procedures for retirement) do not have a very high formative power for the shaping of a person's identity. In comparison to traditional societies, modern industrialized societies are characterized by a low degree of consistency of social demands over time and situations, and thus do not favor stability and continuity of self-experience (Brim and Kagan, 1980). To develop and maintain identity in modern societies means to possess adaptive capacities that enable one to find meaning and satisfaction in heterogeneous situations, conditions, and circumstances of everyday life:

> The actor is to find self-esteem, but not in any fixed moral frame. A sense of efficacy and an internal locus of control are desirable, in unspecified domains. Activity and initiative are appropriate, and shyness and anomie are to be avoided. Effective attachments to an unspecified environment – but attachments only to secure that freedom and independence can be retained – are desiderata, isolation is defeat. . . . The modern self, in other words, is free and is expected to relativize its stance to the institutional context. It seeks to find meaning and value in comparison to the referential structures set by the rationalized environment. (Meyer, 1986, p. 209)

Thus, the demand for "individuation" and "individualization" is very high. The self-concept must, as Meyer puts it, transcend the sequencing features of the life course and is licensed to construct a strong identity that is independent and immunized from the organized social reality. At the same time, social pressure is placed on the capacities of the individual for the coordination and guidance of personal behavior. Separated areas of life, manifested through differentiation into societal subsystems, institutions, and organizations, carry for each individual the danger of losing social identity. Through increasing pressure toward an individualized shaping of biographical transitions, personal identity becomes vulnerable to unpredicted breaks in continuity. The formation and maintenance of a continuity of self-experience is precarious at every point in time during the biography and must repeatedly be newly produced in each concrete situation. It is conceivable that this also leads to an increase in the risk of stress and problem behavior.

DEVIANCE AND PROBLEM BEHAVIOR AS CONSEQUENCES OF UNSUCCESSFUL SOCIALIZATION

The success or failure of socialization is determined by the suitability of a person's action competences, self-concept, and identity formation to the developmental tasks in a given biographical and social situation. If the structure and profile of the behavioral repertoire are not sufficiently developed, there is a risk that psychologically and socially deviant forms of action and behavior will arise that create problems for the continued development of the personality.

As we saw in the preceding section, the scientific explanation of the causes and development of deviant and problem behavior does not differ from the explanation of the nondeviant and unproblematic behavior that is usually classified as "normal." The classification refers to the results and manifestations of the individual confrontation between a person and his or her external and internal reality: If these results conform with societal norms and expectations, the behavior is considered normal; if it does not conform, it is regarded as abnormal.

Therefore, deviant and/or problem behavior is considered to include (1) all behavior that is forbidden by law or that is socially undesirable or unacceptable (whether or not it contradicts prevailing conventions, and whether or not it disrupts the orderly and peaceful coexistence of the members of society), and/or (2) behavior that interferes with or handicaps the development of an individual's personality. The problem with this descriptive definition is that it leaves open the question of by whose criteria behavior will be classified as undesirable or unacceptable. The criteria employed are definitely always those of the most powerful subcultures and social classes in a society. Behavior that does not meet their criteria may be labeled as deviant or problem behavior, even though it may be normal and functional in the appropriate minority subculture.

Manifestations of deviant and problem behavior

Manifestations of deviant and problem behavior are differentiated mostly according to the direction and the extent of their conflict potential: Is the behavior aimed at the social environment or at the person him- or herself? Does it contain aggressive impulses toward other people or oneself? Does it express a protest against social reference persons and groups or a protest against oneself? Does it cause damage to other people or to oneself? These manifestations of behavior can be labeled externally, or "conflict-directed" behavior, as opposed to internally, or "withdrawal-directed" behavior. The most significant manifestations of externally directed abnormal behavior are aggressive, dissocial, delinquent, and criminal forms of behavior, such as violence and injury to other people, disturbance of public order, and destruction of property ("deviant behavior"). The most significant manifestations of internally directed abnormal behavior are health-endangering behavior that harms the body, such as drug consumption, reckless driving, and attempted suicide ("problem behavior"). Between these two poles, there lies a broad spectrum of manifestations of psychosocial and psychosomatic symptoms for disorders of personality development ("behavior disorders") such as learning and achievement disorders, difficulty in making social contacts, and depressive mood, to name just a few.

Deviant and problem behavior can be differentiated from "normal" behavior only in a provisional sense. The demarcations between normal and abnormal behaviors are hard to define, because somatic, psychological, and social disorders occur in various forms and styles and because different criteria of definition and identification are applied to them in each historical epoch. The concepts and terms for the description and analysis of the antecedent conditions and the course of normal and abnormal behavior, as well as the criteria for the degree of deviation a behavior has to show in order to be judged a problem for either the person or society, are dependent on social and cultural conditions (Rutter, 1980).

What is considered deviant and problem behavior also depends on definitions given by the influential authorities of social control, political order, and health care. Whether a behavior is classified as criminal or not, for example, is influenced initially by whether the behavior has even been noticed, then by whether it has been put on record, and finally by whether it has been categorized under the heading of "criminality" (Hirschi, 1969; Brusten and Hurrelmann, 1976).

Similar statements can be made for other manifestations of abnormal behavior: Which behaviors by children will be considered abnormal by parents, teachers, educational counselors, social workers, psychologists, or doctors depends decisively on their respective value orientations, their attitudes toward the particular child, their own psychological dispositions, their professional competence (which is linked to their training), and their professional positions. Great differences can be found, for example, between teachers' and parents' assessments of psychologically or socially abnormal behavior in their children or students, since teachers and parents are affected in different ways by the forms of behavior a child shows. Parents are usually more sensitive to withdrawn and apathetic behavior in their children than are teachers, who pay more attention to the variants of a child's behavior that disturb their teaching activity. Educational counselors, doctors, and psychiatric workers, because of their trained judgment ability, basically show a stronger tendency than parents to perceive all forms of abnormal behavior. Additionally, such factors as professional training, scientific and therapeutic orientation, and the type, size, facilities, and quality of the counseling and care establishments in which they work influence the process of defining what is and what is not classified as problem behavior (Jessor and Jessor, 1977; Mattejat, 1985, p. 18).

Of course, scientific research also cannot escape such biases. The classification of problem behavior in a scientific study is always based on a definition given by the research team. Here too, a decisive role is played by, for instance, the disciplinary orientation of the research group, its theoretical and methodological interests, the institutional commitments of the investigation, and its eventual sponsors. This helps to explain why studies have often produced widely varying findings on the manifestations and distribution of problem behavior. Since most manifestations of problem behavior show no fixed borders separating it from normal behavior, cutoff points are usually denoted in the research process that set the severity, duration, and intensity of a symptom that constitutes the crossover to abnormality and deviance (Petersen and Ebata, 1987).

The advantage of this procedure is that it does not depend upon an absolute conception of normality, and thus avoids any premature pathologization of abnormal forms of behavior. It is based on the theory that, within a broad spectrum of various forms and styles of behavior, problem variants can arise, both individually and societally, that deserve particular attention because they impair individual development and, to some extent, also the coexistence of the members of a social group or unit.

All available studies about the various manifestations of problem behavior and the frequency of their occurrence document an increase in the rates of prevalence and incidence in many fields over the last two decades, not just among children and adolescents but also among adults (Petri, 1979; Rutter, 1980; Bachman,

Successful and unsuccessful socialization

O'Malley, and Johnston, 1982). Although it is hard to tell to what degree this reflects the application of more precise instruments for screening, diagnosis, and assessment (cf. Frankenburg, Emde, and Sullivan, 1985), the research findings nevertheless indicate the need, in future research, for a careful analysis of the underlying facts.

Antecedent conditions for deviant and problem behavior

From the perspective of socialization theory, the major starting point for the emergence of deviant and problem behavior must be seen in the lack of agreement between individual action competences and situative behavioral demands that are shaped by specific organizations and institutions. The quality and the profile of the action competences result from the relation between personal and environmental factors that was discussed in detail in the preceding section.

Thus, a risk constellation for the emergence of problem behavior always exists when, owing to a specific pattern of personal and environmental features, a person lastingly lacks suitable and sufficient action competences, usually accompanied by an unstable and/or distorted self-concept, and cannot provide the abilities and skills that the social environment expects and demands. In such a case, the profile and structure of the person's action competences do not agree with the standards given by societal norms. These standards (as we saw in the first part of this chapter), vary according to biographical and situational factors: Each life phase contains a fixed combination of development tasks that must be mastered if the experience of identity is to occur.

A certain degree of mismatching between individual competences and social demands is a stimulus for continued personality development. If, however, individual competences and the demands made on individual action do not match for a long period of time, and this occurs in an important subarea of the developmental tasks, a constellation exists that must be classified as putting pressure on the individual and endangering the establishment of a "healthy" identity. In psychological and sociological research, the term "stress" has become established as a label for the effects of such pressures: Stress arises if a person experiences a disparity between social demands and claims, on the one

123

hand, and action possibilities on the other, and simultaneously experiences the consequences of this discrepancy as being threatening for the feeling of identity (Lazarus and Launier, 1978; Pearlin, 1983).

A risk constellation for the emergence of stress can also be characterized by a person's having unsuitable or insufficient competence at coordinating the various demands in different fields of activity. Such a situation is essentially much more stressful than the one just mentioned, since the unsuccessful matching and balancing of the demands that are specific to each field of activities overlap. The result can be an identity crisis, since it is no longer just subareas but the entire structure of self-perception and self-appraisal that is involved. To use Antonovsky's term (1979, p. 184), we can say that the individual loses his or her "sense of coherence," that is, "the global orientation that expresses the extent to which one has a pervasive, enduring though dynamic feeling of confidence that one's internal and external environments are predictable and that there is a high probability that things will work out as well as can reasonably be expected."

Whether a specific constellation of stressful situations and events (such as deficits in school and occupational achievement, difficulties in making social contacts, partnership problems, loss of reference persons, or problems with the transition from one phase of life to the next) finds expression in problem behavior depends decisively on specific individual abilities and skills for coping with stress and crisis phenomena. This particularly involves the capacities for self-appraisal and for self-regulation, with its elements of self-control and self-guidance.

If a lack of agreement is perceived between action competences and behavioral demands, individual strategies have to be mobilized to overcome this discrepancy. These strategies can be developed only if the individual is able and willing to perceive his or her personal action competences in a realistic manner and to evaluate and diagnose as exactly as possible in which fields there is a lack of agreement with the behavioral demands of the situation. If this diagnosis is adequate, it should result in the application of strategies to monitor both the individual action competences and the self-concept, with the aim of adjusting them to fit the situation, and – if possible – the situative behavioral demands, in order to remedy the lack of agreement (Pearlin, 1983, 1987, p. 56).

The monitoring strategies mentioned here can be described as coping strategies that are aimed at mastery of stressful social constellations that are specific to a life situation and/or a life phase (Moriarty and Toussieng, 1976; Jessor and Jessor, 1977; Haan, 1981). The more actively a person makes the effort to diagnose a stressful situation and the more flexible he or she is in making corrections and changes, the greater the potential for coping, and the greater the possibility of reducing the pressure without the symptoms of stress appearing in the form of deviance or problem behavior. The more passive the efforts and the more rigid the attempts to guide behavior, the greater the risk that symptoms of stress will appear.

Forms and patterns of strategies of coping behavior have been extensively investigated in recent years. The findings have indicated that coping can be understood as a complex strategy of specific problem-oriented action that makes suitable allowance for situational and biographical conditions and permits the application of realistic, goal-oriented forms of behavior. In most of this research, a distinction is made between "direct" and "indirect" coping strategies. Direct strategies are aimed at changing either personal resources or the situative field of action, whereas indirect ones are aimed exclusively at cognitive, emotional, and motivational reestimation of the existing stress through the regulation of self-related and other attitudes and emotions (Lazarus and Launier, 1978). From the perspective of socialization theory, it is important to supplement this research with studies that analyze the state of identity formation and the overall social context within which coping strategies develop and occur.

Besides individual coping strategies, the social support offered by persons and institutions is an important moderating factor that can decide whether a stressful situation will lead to problem behavior or not. Social support includes both the services of the various state-run, partially state-run, and private specialized institutions of care and welfare, and also the services of the informal social systems of family, relatives, neighbors, groups of friends, and so forth. They all can provide help in specific ways with everyday problem situations and with critical life events. Persons who have flexible and reliable social networks are evidently more resistant to stress than those who do not (Gottlieb, 1983, p. 62). The connections between both formal and informal systems are of great importance. Ideally, they should be cumulatively effective, reciprocally strengthening each other and thus providing a particularly effective contribution to coping with stress (Fischer, 1982).

If we wish to consider all of the potential means of help and support that can be found in the social environment, we have to take into account the entire network of continual interaction patterns and social relationships that can offer support in coping with stress constellations. Attention must be paid to aspects such as the concrete structure of the social network; knowledge about and estimates of the support potential of both formal and informal systems; willingness to accept the help and support of these systems; and the actual utility of the support potential in stress situations. Measures of support are effective if they improve the possibilities for the development of personality or if they uncover buried possibilities of development. In order to do this, they must be applied in such a way that they strengthen individual capacities and strategies for coping with risk constellations (Gottlieb, 1983).

Not only the emergence but also the further development of deviant and problem behavior, as well as its consolidation and reinforcement in the form of a "deviant career," depend on the presence and strength of two modifying and moderating factors: individual coping strategies that activate monitoring capacties, and the support potential of the social environment, which can check and balance stressful situations and risk factors and, simultaneously, strengthen the capacity for coping. A precondition for the activation of coping strategies – and probably also for the suitable tapping and use of the support potential of the social environment – is the presence of the abilities of self-perception and self-appraisal that influences the potential to control and monitor personal action.

Figure 4.1 illustrates a model of the conditioning and moderating factors for deviant and problem behavior in adolescence. The model consists of several steps that lead to the emergence and consolidation of deviant and problem behavior and lists, as potential moderating factors, individual style of managing and coping and social support. This model can be applied to other phases of life with their appropriate developmental tasks, transitional demands, and risk factors.

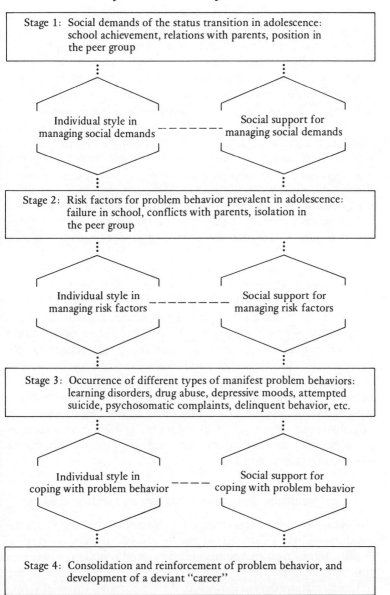

Figure 4.1. Model of the genesis and development of problem behavior in adolescence.

Social structure and personality development

We need more investigations into the balancing, neutralizing, and aggravating effects of specific forms of coping and specific forms of support. It is evident that there are no simple linear cause-and-effect relations among the various factors but complicated, reciprocal nets of relations. Future research must pay particular attention to why different degrees and levels of normal and abnormal behavior can occur with different persons, even though the antecedent conditions are the same. For example, experience shows that there are cases in which an extremely unfavorable constellation of antecedent conditions does not lead to problem behavior. A more exact investigation of such unexpected constellations promises increased understanding of the conditions that lead to problem behavior (Silbereisen and Eyferth, 1986).

Another point of some theoretical importance will also require much attention in future research: How is identity influenced by the emergence of problem behavior, and what effect does the process of identity formation have on the process of the emergence of problem behavior? We can anticipate that when deviance reaches serious proportions it will lead to an identity disorder, because it must cause fundamental subjective uncertainties about the continuity of self-experience. A disordered identity formation probably has, in turn, repercussions on the development of problem behavior. On the other hand, when deviance reaches serious proportions, it may result in the taking of a deviant identity, through almost complete personal identification and association with a deviant subgroup (as among many drug users). This must be considered to be a problematic way of resolving, at least temporarily, uncertainties about the continuity of self-experience (Rosenberg, 1981, p. 621).

Living conditions, familial socialization, and problem behavior

For many years now, researchers have attempted to investigate the relations between features of the living conditions, as well as familial interaction and communication, and problem behavior in children and adolescents. In general, the results have shown a significant relation between unfavorable social and material living conditions (such as material poverty, an unfavorable residential situation, and an unfavorable structure of leisure opportunities in the residential area) and the frequent occurrence of various manifestations of problem behavior, such as learning disorders, dissocial behavior, drug use, and delinquency. There are also significant correlations between problem behavior and such features as incomplete family, emotionally tense marriage partner relationship, parental violence toward children, and lack of emotional care (Schneewind, Beckmann, and Engfer, 1983, p. 38; Garbarino, Schellenbach, and Sebes, 1986).

However, none of these relations is direct and linear, and they do not follow the pattern of cause and effect. For this reason, it is difficult to obtain statements about the relations between life situations and abnormality and/or deviance that have a general validity. Nevertheless, the available studies provide rough pointers for a relation between social and material disadvantage and problem behavior.

It is evident that the stresses that children, adolescents, and adults face in socially and materially disadvantaged families are harder for them to master than is the case in other families. It would appear that the forms and strategies that they have for coping with stress and for organizing social support are less efficient. In families that generally have positive experiences when coping with life's demands, we can observe a stronger resistance to threats to mental health when stress and critical life events occur. Another reason for the differences in the processing of stress can be seen in the fact that members of socially privileged families have more economic resources and more power and influence at their command, with which they are better able to handle risk factors or turn to other possibilities of gaining satisfaction (Laosa and Sigel, 1982; Vondra, 1986).

These and other factors can lead, in disadvantaged families, to a negative subjective perception of social reality that greatly limits the scope for coping strategies. An impairment of the abilities for processing reality aggravates the confrontation with difficulties and increases the risk of also reacting to stress situations with psychological symptoms. However, the relation between features of social status and behavioral difficulties cannot be interpreted as a direct relation. It is not individual factors from the spectrum of living conditions or familial (or school, occupational, or other) interaction conditions that are the causes of deviant and problem behavior. Rather, the effect of each single factor (such as material poverty, residence in a shelter for the homeless, or a broken marriage relation) is decided according to the accompanying circumstances – in particular, the coping strategies and the social support activities, whose presence or absence possibly has either a weakening or strengthening effect. Whether a single stressful factor leads to problem behavior is decided by the context in which this factor is embedded.

For example, the educational attitudes and practices of the parents should not be looked at in isolation. In itself, the practice applied has little predictive value, although it may reflect the type of relationship that exists between the child and the parents. It is not only that which is done but the relational frame in which it occurs and the aspects of a relationship that are expressed in an educational activity that are of significance. The educational style and the general attitude toward the child are more significant than the particular educational practice. Children's behavioral disorders do not develop out of the individual mistakes that parents make when educating their children but from a disturbed relationship as a whole. Individual educational practices must therefore be seen within the entire context of the relationship between the parents and the child (Garbarino, 1982).

Additionally, a child or adolescent not only experiences familial relationships in direct interaction with the mother and father but also through a subjective perception of the parents' relationship. The feeling that the child or adolescent has regarding the security and stability of his or her space for development in the family is directly influenced by his or her experience of the parental relationship. If mother–child interactions or father–child interactions are to be studied with a view to the children's personality development, then particular attention must be paid to the emotional quality of the relationships and the degree of control and influence.

Previous investigations into educational practices show that behavioral disorders of the conflict-directed (aggressive) type are related to a lack of emotional warmth and hostile, rejecting, and punitive parental behavior. The aspect of control must always be related to the emotional relationship between the parents and their child. Aggressive behavior disorders are accompanied by an accumulation of punitive, position-oriented, and power-related attempts at parental control, and there is a lack of effective parental supervision and guidance. It is also evident that inconsequent and inconsistent educational behavior and a lack of agreement between the parents encourages the development of aggressive and dissocial behavior. In contrast, behavioral disorders of the withdrawal-directed (inhibited) type are more often found in connection with anxious, uncertain, partially overprotective, and rejecting parental educational behavior (Mattejat, 1985, p. 107).

As this review has shown, the relations between living conditions, social interaction, and communication, and deviant and problem behavior must be more closely analyzed in future research, and particular attention must be paid to the risk constellations and the modifying factors mentioned. In order to trace the nature of the process by which forms of problem behavior develop, it is necessary to combine case analysis methods for the reconstruction of an entire system of relations with survey procedures for the analysis of the interconnections between specific variables (cf. the methodological propositions listed in chapter 3).

Gender-specific aspects

Future research must also undertake a much more intensive consideration of gender-specific differences. All of the studies produced to date show gender-specific differences in levels of problem behavior, with a greater prevalence of conflict-directed behavior of all varieties observed for male children, adolescents, and adults than for females, particularly in the area of delinquent and criminal behavior. In the area of behavioral disorders, males also show a markedly higher average frequency than females, which is particularly noticeable in disorders in learning and achievement behavior. This general trend also extends into the field of behavior that endangers health.

Many theories assume that males and females interpret and relate to their environment differently, and try to explain this through psychological and biological differences between the sexes (Gilligan, 1982). In fact, the substantial changes in the social roles of females are not reflected in analogous changes in the rates of deviant behavior relative to the rates of males. As Gove (1985) notes, the gender difference in deviant behavior seems to be sufficiently stable across time and place so that it cannot be explained directly by changes in the structure of society or sex-role socialization. Although for females, as for males, late adoles-

cence is marked by a lack of social orientation, normative guidance, and clear responsibilities, males and females cope with this
situation in different ways:

> The psychological well-being of both males and females is at a low
> point during adolescence and early adulthood. Young females are
> more self-absorbed, uncooperative, distrustful, and willing to act
> in socially unacceptable ways than older females, although the dif-
> ference with age is not nearly so sharp for males. Furthermore,
> physical strength and energy tend to peak at approximately the
> same age for males and females. . . . [Nevertheless,] the affiliative
> orientation of females and their concern for the impact of their
> behavior on others should significantly limit their interest, desire,
> and/or willingness to commit deviant acts. In contrast, the inde-
> pendent, assertive personality of males is much more compatible
> with a willingness to be involved in deviant behavior. (Gove, 1985,
> pp. 137–8)

It is important to note that the low rates of deviant behavior
among females cannot be attributed to low rates of psychological
distress. On the contrary, female adolescents and young adults are
more likely to experience psychological distress, particularly
expressed in symptoms of psychosomatic disorders, than males
(Hurrelmann, Engel, Holler, and Nordlohne, 1988). Additionally, in some areas prevalence rates of internally oriented, self-
aggressive, and health-endangering behavior (e.g., depressive
mood, attempted suicide, anorexia nervosa, abuse of pharmaceut-
ical products) for girls and women are higher than for boys and
men (Rutter, 1980, p. 88).

Certainly, previous research does not yet provide sufficient support for the proposition that girls have a completely different way
of processing and managing internal and external reality from
boys. However, the major difference in manifest deviant and
problem behavior is that the average frequency of all types of
aggressive, conflict-oriented behavior is higher among boys. This
means that the determinable differences in social behavior lie on
the dimension of social influence, power, and super- or sub-ordi-
nation. The behavior of girls and boys in the area of aggression is
lastingly influenced by the power relationships and the abuse of
power in their surrounding adult society. In a society in which
both the public and private exercise of violence is predominantly
the domain of males, these differences in the behavior of children

must be understood as steps in the learning of the norms of our culture (Hagemann-White, 1984, p. 45).

The economic, social, and cultural division of labor between the sexes must be regarded as a decisive factor in female and male socialization. This guides the society's ideas on social roles and attitudes toward masculinity and femininity and finally leads to the formation of life spaces that differ according to sex within the same society, the same family, the same school class, and so forth (Rossi, 1985). A warning must be given against a mechanical explanation of gender-specific variations in behavior. Future research will be involved in analyzing the gender-specific forms of the acquisition and productive processing of external and internal reality. In other words, we must ask in what way, and in what fields, different patterns of interaction with the social and material environment that lead to different forms of normal and abnormal behavior can be explained by the sex variable.

INTERVENTIONS IN THE PROCESS OF SOCIALIZATION

The increase in our scientific understanding of the process of socialization has been accompanied by a growth in our knowledge about how we can use purposeful interventions to influence the personality development of an individual. *Environment-centered interventions* are predominantly performed by shaping the social and material living conditions and the structures of interaction and communication in the organizations, institutions, and groups that are relevant for socialization. *Person-centered interventions* are predominantly educational, psychological, and therapeutic interventions in the individual's processing of external and internal reality.

The more precisely we understand the conditions and processes of socialization, the more effectively we can apply these kinds of interventions. They raise far-reaching questions, not only regarding the way they really function and their actual effectiveness – which in many cases is still unexplained – but also regarding their legitimacy (Kaufmann, 1987). As I have continually tried to argue in this book, interventions are ethically, politically, and educationally legitimate only if they encourage the personality development of a person and improve the preconditions for the success of socialization.

Socialization theory should on no account exclude such questions from its domain. On the contrary, it must take full responsibility for them. For this reason, this final section deals with the problems involved in intervention.

The concepts of intervention and prevention

The term "intervention" has become a collective name for a multitude of measures that are applied to avoid the development of deviant and problem behavior, to counteract the consolidation of such behavior, and to block its side effects (Hurrelmann, Kaufmann, and Lösel, 1987). The term "prevention" is widely used to distinguish measures that are directed at completely avoiding the occurrence of deviant and problem behavior. Prevention describes all the measures that are administered, in anticipation of problems, at a point in time when impairment and damage to the development of personality is predictable but has yet to occur. Thus, preventive measures are directed at the potential antecedent conditions for stressful situations and events and, in a strict sense, are of a prophylactic nature (Brandtstädter and van Eye, 1982; Seidman, 1983; Edelstein and Michelson, 1986).

The term prevention has been used extensively in the psychological and medical literature of recent years. The conceptual demarcation into primary, secondary, and tertiary prevention has been introduced to differentiate among different stages of intervention (Caplan and Grunebaum, 1967; Cowen, 1983). The term "primary prevention" covers all of the measures and practices that are applied to the antecedent personal and social conditions before the occurrence of any symptoms of problem behavior, in order to prevent the emergence of such a behavior. "Secondary prevention" describes those measures that permit an early diagnosis of symptoms, with the aim of an early intervention the first time the symptoms occur, in order to shorten the duration of problem behavior. Finally, "tertiary prevention" describes those measures that are applied after the occurrence of symptoms of problem behavior and are meant to lessen any further consolidation of symptoms and also reduce harmful side effects in other fields of behavior.

I have some reservations about the extensive use of the term prevention. The conceptual demarcation just described classifies prevention according to the point in time when an intervention is applied. Consequently, the term prevention should be used only for those measures that are applied prophylactically *before* the occurrence of any manifestation of problem behavior (stages 1 and 2 in Figure 4.1), whereas all other measures that are applied *after* the occurrence and diagnosis of problem behavior (stages 3 and 4 in Figure 4.1) should no longer be covered by the term. There is much to be said for reserving the term prevention exclusively for those interventions that are labeled "primary prevention" or "secondary prevention" in the medical and psychological tradition. All measures that do not meet the criterion of preventive intervention should, in contrast, be categorized as "postventive" or "corrective" interventions (Hurrelmann, 1987a).

We should use the term "preventive intervention" to denote all measures directed toward an improvement in personal well-being and social living conditions of a person or group of persons in order to prevent the occurrence of risk constellations leading to problem behavior. These measures are aimed at the prevention of all known personal and social conditions that lead to problem behavior, including the social demands of status transition. In this sense, the term "preventive intervention" is used synonymously with the term "primary prevention." Additionally, we can use the term "preventive intervention" to designate all measures that focus on already recognizable, concrete signs of those social conditions that indisputably contain a high risk for the occurrence of problem behavior. This form of intervention is aimed at reducing the expected effects of the risk factors, in order to minimize the possibility of problem behavior occurring. Thus, we are dealing here with measures that are aimed at selectively anticipating a potential development toward problem behavior. These measures are often combined with a screening procedure that examines whether or not the first symptoms related to maladjusted behavior are present. In this sense, the term "preventive intervention" is, to some degree, used synonymously with the term "secondary prevention."

We should use the term "corrective intervention" to designate measures that focus on already existing problem behavior and that attempt to prevent further development or reinforcement of the problem behavior. These measures are implemented when the problem behavior is clearly visible in a recognizable form. Thus, it can be seen that these are not prophylactic measures (in contrast to the measures described earlier) but rather measures that are responses to the occurrence of problem behavior and are intended to correct it. This range of measures includes those that attempt to limit or avoid the further consolidation of problem behavior and, in particular, its destructive side effects in other areas. In this sense, the term "corrective intervention" is, to a certain degree, used synonymously with the term "tertiary prevention."

I suggest the use of these terms, rather than "primary prevention," "secondary prevention," and "tertiary prevention," because they make it abundantly clear that all the measures discussed are measures of intervention – that is, actions that interfere. However, as previously mentioned, there are many close links between the two terminologies that permit us to recognize a joint concept, namely, classifying and finding forms of intervention that correspond to the different stages in the development of deviant and problem behavior shown in Figure 4.1.

We can derive some general principles for intervention practices within the understanding sketched here from the basic approach to socialization theory that I have emphasized in this book. The focus of all intervention practices must be directed toward influencing both environmental (social) resources and personal resources, and also the interaction between both of these groups of factors. This requires both measures that focus on the individual and are applied directly to the persons concerned, and socially oriented measures that relate to the environment in which the persons are placed.

Measures that focus on the individual must essentially aim to encourage the action competence of the person in such a way as to enable appropriate coping with the demands of the social environment. Socially oriented practices of intervention must be designed with the aim of altering the form of the social and material environment so that a person can cope with it with the action competence at his or her command. By influencing both the environment and the person, it must become possible for a person to cope with a situation in which there is a discrepancy between behavioral demands and the competences available, because the competences have been changed, and, simultaneously, the structurally determined behavioral demands have been influenced.

Accordingly, the general aim of all measures of intervention must be to arrange the discrepancies between individual action competences and strategies for coping with situations, on the one hand, and social demands from the environment on the other hand, in a form that is manageable for the individual person. Thus, essential starting points for intervention measures are the strengthening of the social support potential of the formal and informal systems in the social environment, and the strengthening of the action competence for coping with the situative social demands (Gottlieb, 1983, p. 28).

Possibilities and potentials of prevention

The great opportunities for preventive activities lie in avoiding unnecessary pressures on a person from the outset and excluding the damaging and impairing consequences of stressful situations and events.

First, all information and communciation strategies aimed at the explanation of the emergence of stress belong to the repertoire of preventive measures (Edelstein and Michelson, 1986). For example, educators and teachers should have at their command a comprehensive understanding of the conditions that bring about and consolidate disorders in personality development. Such explanatory instruction could be carried out for preventive purposes in all areas of education and vocational training, as well as in the mass media. It should, in particular, be intensively aimed at those occupational groups that continually have to deal with children and adolescents and in whom an accurate knowledge of the possible antecedent conditions for deviant and problem behavior could have the largest multiplicative effect.

Second, the entire spectrum of sociopolitical measures to improve the living conditions of children, adolescents, and adults in the economic, social, and cultural field is decisive for strategies of preventive intervention. If we look at adolescence, examples of preventive intervention can be seen in measures for improving the personal well-being and self-image of individuals, on the one hand, and measures for improving social living conditions on the other. Improvement in social living conditions can refer to all of the areas described in the second section of this chapter – namely, improvement in the resources and the quality of education and school, of the interaction within the family, and of the possibilities for strengthening and expanding contacts among members of the peer group. In this sense, the category of preventive intervention has a very broad scope: All those general measures concerning school, family, and social policies for adolescents that promise an improvement in their general living conditions can be included here. The advantage of these measures lies in their prophylactic character: Interventions are made before a process in which problem behavior could occur has even the chance of developing. It is for this reason that preventive measures must be considered to be among the most effective measures, since they attack the actual breeding ground for problem behavior itself (Albee, 1987).

Third, measures of preventive intervention can be based on well-founded assumptions about risk factors in the development of problem behavior, measures that address stage 2 in the model presented in Figure 4.1. If, for example, we consider the area of educational training in adolescence, the scope of the measures stretches from individual support for improving academic achievements to the introduction of flexible teaching methods that are sensitive to the learning style of individual students. Concerning risk factors in the family, we have to consider, for example, measures of dynamic group therapy that involve all members of the family. With regard to the peer group, we can include measures for improving the social integration of school classes and youth groups. On this level of preventive intervention it is important that the risk constellations for individuals and groups of adolescents be recognized as early as possible, so that appropriate measures for countering these risk constellations can be taken, in order to prevent the occurrence of deviant and problem behavior (Silbereisen, Noack, and Reitzle, 1987).

Limitations and potential dangers of prevention

As we have seen, preventive intervention that aims to avoid the emergence of symptoms of problem behavior can be applied successfully only where there is sufficient understanding of the antecedent conditions, the risk factors, and the form of development of problem behavior. Yet, as the discussion of deviance and problem behavior has clearly shown, sufficient understanding is available in only a few subareas. Thus, prevention often consists of tentative attempts that touch on a broad spectrum of conditional factors without being able to claim any certainty of success. For these reasons, in practice, intervention measures usually do not focus on preventive actions in the strict sense but on the earliest possible interventions that are applied after the very first symptoms of problem behavior have occurred.

Is there any justification for not completely exploiting all possible preventive opportunities? To answer this question, we must not only carefully analyze the potentials and possibilities but also the dangers of prevention. We can recognize danger areas that must be taken into consideration in the social, psychological, and educational fields of action.

First, a one-sided concentration on prevention strategies unequally shifts attention to the antecedent conditions of deviant and problem behavior. This is often linked to the basic assumption that it is particularly conditions in early childhood that decisively determine the course of the later phases of life. Such a focus of attention, however, lacks empirical support when we consider the potential for change that is found over the entire life span (discussed in chapter 3 in the section on occupational and adult socialization). No social scientist is in a position to make unequivocal and clear predictions about the development of personality. As we have noted, extremely unfavorable constellations of living conditions can be present without resulting in problem behavior. We are at best able to produce statements about the probability of the occurrence of psychosocial and psychosomatic disorders and deviations throughout the life span.

Second, a concentration on preventive strategies may focus both theoretical and practical attention on the risk groups possessing features that have a certain probability of leading to psychosocial and psychosomatic disorders. A concentration of intervention resources on risk groups that have been selected according to probability criteria may carry the implication that other groups are neglected. Prevention strategies that concentrate only on risk groups violate the central idea of prevention that, for *all* persons, social living conditions must be realized in which support potential and individual action competences are adequate for coping with social demands, to ensure a healthy personal development.

Third, an exaggerated fixation on preventive measures can lead to a false conception of healthy personality development. It would be a mistake to understand prevention as meaning that all the antecedent conditions for the occurrence of discrepancies between situative demands and individual competences should be completely cleared away. A certain degree of discrepancy between demands and competences is a precondition for the further development of personality, since it represents a challenge to mobilize personal and social resoures. The aim is not to totally avoid the occurrence of potential stress but to achieve those conditions that permit a management of stressful situations if they should occur. Each intervention must be directed toward strengthening the developmental process of a personality by encouraging the potentials for effective coping with situational and developmental tasks. In no case should prevention weaken an individual's competence to confront stressful situations and events effectively.

Finally, there is a methodological problem: The more purposeful the prevention strategies that are applied to risk groups, the more intensively must data and information be recorded in order to systematically identify risk groups. The recording of such data could rapidly violate and cross the borders of informational self-determination. In the search for the causes of problem behavior, the recording of data from the private sphere of an individual is unavoidable, for example, if the researcher wants to identify those destructive family relationships that could lead to child and juvenile delinquency. A dangerous side effect of preventive measures in the field of social, psychological, and educational practice can thus lie in an encroachment into the private sphere of a family that cannot be limited to scientific purposes if a risk is detected.

Analyses of the conditions and more precise analyses of the effects of single measures are important for future discussion of the effectiveness of prevention. Until these are available, it is advisable for public authorities to maintain a critical attitude toward preventive measures.

Social intervention in educational fields

The central aim of intervention strategies in educational fields must be to emancipate and strengthen the individual's competences and to activate social support. This aim can be approached in a number of ways and with various forms of intervention, such as instruction, behavioral training, and counseling. In this final section of the book, we will examine the limits and potential of some of these forms of intervention that are of outstanding relevance for the process of socialization.

1. In general, in educational fields of action such as kindergartens and schools, educators must have the necessary competence to diagnose and identify various symptoms of deviant and problem behavior and be able to assess the manifestations of situations that bring about stress and crises. Along with this diagnostic capacity, a suitable practical ability to apply this knowledge must be available. The professional competence of educators consists of a combination of these two factors.

2. A fundamental principle of every intervention measure in the tradition of socialization theory, as it has been presented here, must be to respect and strengthen the individual's autonomy and to regard children and adolescents as the subjects of actions who apply meaningful resources in order to attain specific goals and as responsible persons who are potentially capable of making their own decisions. As a consequence, the educator ideally needs to use no other forms of influence than the presentation of arguments that specify goals, means, and consequences. The "clients" are not subjected to treatment without their expressed consent, and they are not exposed to socioecological context conditions in which they are not able to control the effects. Therefore, educational interventions support the ability of the client to make his or her own rational and emotional decisions.

3. The goal of the educator must be to ensure that a child or adolescent attains the status of a subject who is autonomously capable of both action and the experience of identity. In the case of behavioral problems, children and adolescents should receive temporary assistance in processing reality and building up their individual action competence, until such time as they possess the capacity to guide and interpret their own actions. That is to say, educators and teachers must apply their professional competence in such a way that it leads to the construction or reestablishment of the children's and adolescents' action competence. In this sense, educators must function as guardians and counselors who possess the professional competence to help children and adolescents learn to help themselves and to free and uncover their retarded or buried competences. The communicative structure of instruction, training, and counseling in educational fields is ideally a discourse in which educator and client attempt to find a common solution to problems and thereby cultivate an interaction in which both parties have equal rights and that is as free of sanctions as possible.

4. Particular emphasis must be placed on a nondiscriminatory and nonstigmatizing approach to deviant and problem behavior. This requires that educators and teachers possess the ability to appreciate the interpretations of problems that children and adolescents make themselves, to understand them sympathetically, and to offer their own interpretations of the problem for consideration. The first law of educational action toward children and adolescents must be to avoid a consolidation of deviant and problem behavior once it has occurred and to activate the possibilities of normalizing behavior by offering problem-solving training and informational instruction and by presenting counterdefinitions, new interpretations of situations, and proposals for the removal of self-imposed blocks on the productive processing of reality.

5. In order to realize the central target of any social intervention, namely, to construct and/or reconstruct a person's action competence, the educator's activities must be directed not only toward the person of the client but toward the social and material environment as well. The aim must be to produce the environmental conditions that can best function as a favorable social context for coping with life's demands. To the extent that corresponding possibilities for development are not available in other fields, the educational fields of kindergarten and school must fulfill a complementary role.

6. Social intervention in educational fields has to address both the individual (the client) and his or her environment. Any form of preventive or corrective intervention is basically directed at supporting children and adolescents in developing and exploiting

those behavioral abilities that will place them in a position in which they are able to interact effectively and productively with the demands of the environment. Any concentration of intervention measures on the person of the client quickly reaches the limits of its effectiveness if the entire social structure of the environment, and, in particular, the teacher–student relationship, which is essential for the transformation and mediation of these environmental demands, is not included in the measures. Therefore, educators, teachers, school principals, and the staff of educational institutions as a group have to be included in intervention procedures (Johnson, 1986, p. 135).

7. The same holds for the parents. Many of the manifestations of the problem behavior of children and adolescents that arise in kindergartens and schools have their origin in the family interaction, where they have not been resolved (Epstein, 1987). This often involves parent–child contradictions in perspectives on and aspirations for the child's progress in school and occupation, expectations regarding leisure time activities, and ideas about peer contacts. Forms of problem behavior are also often seen in school that indicate tense and emotionally unsatisfying relationships among the members of the family (Youniss, 1980).

Family intervention has a particularly important position in the entire policy of social, psychological, and educational intervention because its effects are multiplicative. When it is successful, family intervention influences the most important authority for socialization in childhood and adolescence, and at the same time it also influences the most important social and emotional reference group for adults: the family. This is the main reason why in recent years the field of family intervention, particularly in the context of strategies that strengthen the family's position in the community ("empowerment strategies"), has been both conceptually and organizationally expanded (Cochran, 1987).

8. In order to design effective educational interventions, we must particularly reconsider the significance of the school within the social network of contacts and support during childhood and adolescence. To the extent that the school enriches its educational activities through the competent application of preventive and corrective interventions, it can, alongside and in cooperation with youth services, become an even more central component of the social network in adolescence and an important part of the youth

counseling system (Hamilton, 1984). An important task in the development of intervention concepts is to dismantle the divisions between support functions in schools and support functions outside of schools and to strengthen the cooperation among all providers of educational intervention:

> To make secondary schools more beneficial influences on adolescent development, we need to expand the variety of roles, relations, and activities adolescents engage in and to create opportunities for adolescents to interact with people of a wider range of ages and cultural backgrounds. This entails opening up the schools to the larger community and the developmental experience it can provide; increasing the efficiency and effectiveness of academic instruction through fuller use of current and emerging instructional technology; giving more attention to the carryover of school learning to other settings; and enlisting the support of the home, community, peer group, and workplace for the developmental functions of schools. (Hamilton, 1984, p. 245)

9. Because peer relations are egalitarian in their communicative quality and contain a large residual of reciprocity (give-and-take), they function as models and reinforcers of personality development in childhood and adolescence. In education, peer reinforcement and support can be used directly and indirectly to promote social competence, and peer modeling to modify the nature of a child's social repertoire (Hartup, 1984, p. 378). For example, peer tutoring has a long history in educational practice. It utilizes the potential existing in peer interaction for constructive educational ends, augments the effort of educators, and enhances the social competences of both the peer tutor and the peer tutee: "Such experiences can enhance self-esteem and change attitudes toward authority figures, the school, and society. Tutoring also provides role-taking opportunities, assists in the acquisition of helping behaviors, and effects a general attitude change concerning nurturance and sympathetic behavior" (Hartup, 1984, p. 381).

10. For the future, we require a combined system of educational, legal, economic, psychological, psychiatric, therapeutic, and medicinal interventions to stimulate and strengthen the developmental potential in important phases of the life cycle and to influence the social, ecological, and material living conditions with their key importance for the development of a healthy personality. The aim of such a comprehensive intervention policy, with an integrated concept of various interrelated strategies and measures, must be to help to ensure individually and collectively successful processes of socialization.

REFERENCES

Abrahams, F. F., & Sommerkorn, I. N. (1976). Arbeitswelt, Familienstruktur und Sozialisation. In K. Hurrelmann (Ed.), *Sozialisation und Lebenslauf*, pp. 70–89. Reinbek, West Germany: Rowohlt.

Albee, G. W. (1987). Powerlessness, politics, and prevention. In K. Hurrelmann, F. X. Kaufmann, & F. Lösel (Eds.), *Social intervention: Potential and constraints*, pp. 37–52. New York: De Gruyter.

Antonovsky, A. (1979). *Health, stress, and coping.* San Francisco: Jossey-Bass.

Archer, M. (1979). *Social origins of educational systems.* London: Sage.

Bachman, J., O'Malley, P., & Johnston, J. (1982). *Youth in transition* (Vol. 6). Ann Arbor: University of Michigan Press.

Baltes, P. B., & Brim, O. (Eds.). (1979). *Life span development and behavior* (Vol. 2). New York: Academic Press.

Baltes, P. B., Dittmann-Kohli, F., & Dixon, R. A. (1986). Multidisciplinary propositions on the development of intelligence during adulthood and old age. In A. B. Sorensen, F. E. Weinert, & L. R. Sherrod (Eds.), *Human development and the life course*, pp. 467–507. Hillsdale, N.J.: Erlbaum.

Baltes, P. B., Reese, H. W., & Lipsitt, L. (1980). Life-span developmental psychology. *American Review of Psychology, 31,* 65–110.

Bandura, A. (1977). *Social learning theory.* Englewood Cliffs: Prentice-Hall.

Bandura, A. (1986). *Social foundations of thought and action.* London: Allen & Unwin.

Baumrind, D. (1978). Parental disciplinary patterns and social competence in children. *Youth and Society, 9,* 193–209.

Berger, P. L., & Luckmann, T. (1967). *The social construction of reality.* New York: Doubleday.

Bernstein, B. (1971). *Class, codes and control* (Vol. 1). London: Routledge & Kegan Paul.

Bernstein, B. (1975). *Class, codes, and control* (Vol. 3). London: Routledge & Kegan Paul.

References

Bertram, H. (1981). *Sozialstruktur und Sozialisation*. Darmstadt: Luchterhand.

Biddle, B., Bank, B. J., & Marlin, M. M. (1980). Parental and peer influence on adolescents. *Social Forces, 58,* 1057–1079.

Bidwell, C. E. (1965). The school as a formal organization. In J. G. March, (Ed.), *Handbook of organizations,* pp. 972–1022. Chicago: Rand-McNally.

Blumer, H. (1969). *Symbolic interactionism: Perspective and method.* Englewood Cliffs: Prentice-Hall.

Bogdan, R., & Taylor, S. J. (1975). *Introduction to qualitative research methods.* New York: Wiley.

Borman, K. M. (Ed.). (1982). *The social life of children in a changing society.* Hillsdale, N.J.: Erlbaum.

Bourdieu, P. (1984). *Distinction: A social critique of the judgment of taste.* London: Routledge & Kegan Paul.

Bourdieu, P., & Passeron, J. C. (1977). *Reproduction in education, society, and culture.* Beverly Hills: Sage.

Brandtstädter, J., & Eye, A. von (Eds.). (1982). *Psychologische Prävention.* Bern: Huber.

Brim, O. G., & Kagan, J. (1980). *Constancy and change in human development.* Cambridge, Mass.: Harvard University Press.

Brim, O. G., & Wheeler, S. (Eds.). (1966). *Socialization after childhood.* New York: Wiley.

Bronfenbrenner, U. (1958). Socialization through time and space. In E. E. Maccoby, T. Newcomb, & E. Hartley (Eds.), *Readings in social psychology* (3rd ed.), pp. 400–425. New York.

Bronfenbrenner, U. (1977). Toward an experimental ecology of human development. *American Psychologist, 32,* 513–531.

Bronfenbrenner, U. (1978). The social role of the child in ecological perspective. *Zeitschrift für Soziologie, 7,* 4–20.

Bronfenbrenner, U. (1979). *The ecology of human development: Experiments by nature and design.* Cambridge, Mass.: Harvard University Press.

Brusten, M., & Hurrelmann, K. (1976). *Abweichendes Verhalten in der Schule.* Munich: Juventa.

Busch, H. J. (1985). *Interaktion und innere Natur: Sozialisationstheoretische Reflexionen.* Frankfurt: Campus.

Bush, D., & Simmons, R. G. (1981). Socialization process over the life course. In M. Rosenberg & R. H. Turner (Eds.), *Social psychology: Sociological perspectives,* pp. 133–164. New York: Basic Books.

Caplan, G., & Grunebaum, H. (1967). Perspectives on primary prevention: A review. *Archives in Genetic Psychiatry, 17,* 331–346.

References

Carnoy, M., & Levin, H. M. (1985). *Schooling and work in the democratic state*. Stanford: Stanford University Press.

Clausen, J. A. (1968). A historical and comparative view of socialization theory and research. In J. A. Clausen (Ed.), *Socialization and society*, pp. 18–72. Boston: Little, Brown.

Clausen, J. A. (1975). The social meaning of differential physical and sexual maturation. In S. Dragastin & G. H. Elder (Eds.), *Adolescence in the life cycle*, pp. 25–49. Washington, D.C.: Hemisphere.

Clausen, J. A. (1981). Men's occupational careers in the middle years. In D. E. Eichorn, J. A. Clausen, N. Haan, M. P. Honzik, & P. Mussen (Eds.), *Present and past in middle life*, pp. 321–355. New York: Academic Press.

Clausen, J. A. (1986a). Early adult choices and the life course. *Zeitschrift für Sozialisationsforschung und Erziehungssoziologie, 6*, 313–321.

Clausen, J. A. (1986b). *The life course*. Englewood Cliffs: Prentice-Hall.

Cochran, M. (1987). Empowering families: An alternative to the deficit model. In K. Hurrelmann, F. X. Kaufmann, & F. Lösel (Eds.), *Social intervention: Potential and constraints*, pp. 105–120. New York: De Gruyter.

Coleman, J. C. (1980). *The nature of adolescence*. London: Methuen.

Coleman, J. S. (1982). *The asymmetric society*. Syracuse: Syracuse University Press.

Collins, R. (1979). *The credential society: A historical sociology of education and stratification*. New York: Academic Press.

Cottrell, L. S. (1969). Interpersonal interaction and the development of the self. In D. Goslin (Ed.), *Handbook of socialization theory and research*, pp. 543–570. Chicago: Rand McNally.

Cowen, E. L. (1983). Primary prevention in mental health: Past, present, and future. In R. D. Felmer et al. (Eds.), *Preventive psychology*, pp. 11–25. New York: Pergamon Press.

Cranach, M. von, Kalbermatten, U., Indermühle, K., & Gugler, B. (1982). *Goal-directed action*. London: Academic Press.

Dahrendorf, R. (1959). *Class and class conflict in industrial society*. Stanford: Stanford University Press.

Damon, W. (1977). *The social world of the child*. San Francisco: Jossey-Bass.

Denzin, N. K. (1977). *Childhood socialization*. San Francisco: Jossey-Bass.

Denzin, N. K. (1978). *The research act* (2nd ed.). New York: McGraw-Hill.

DiMaggio, P. (1982). Cultural capital and school success. *American Sociological Review, 47*, 189–201.

Dohrenwend, B. S., & Dohrenwend, B. P. (1974). *Stressful life events: Their nature and effects*. New York: Wiley.

References

Doise, W., & Palmonari, A. (Eds.). (1984). *Social interaction and individual development*. Cambridge: Cambridge University Press.

Dollase, R. (1985). *Entwicklung und Erziehung*. Stuttgart: Klett.

Durkheim, E. (1968). *Education and sociology*. New York: Free Press.

Eckensberger, L. (1979). A metamethodological evaluation of psychological theories from a cross-cultural perspective. In L. Eckensberger, W. J. Lanner, & Y. H. Poortinga (Eds.), *Cross-cultural contributions to psychology*, pp. 255–275. Lisse: Sweets.

Edelstein, W., & Habermas, J. (Eds.). (1984). *Soziale Interaktion und soziales Verstehen*. Frankfurt: Suhrkamp.

Edelstein, B. A., & Michelson, L. (Eds.). (1986). *Handbook of prevention*. New York: Plenum.

Eichorn, D., Clausen, J. A., Haan, N., Honzik, M. P., & Mussen, P. H. (Eds.). (1984). *Present and past in middle life*. New York: Academic Press.

Elder, G. H. (1974). *Children of the great depression: Social change in life experience*. Chicago: University of Chicago Press.

Elder, G. H. (Ed.). (1979). Historical change in life patterns and personality. In P. H. Baltes & O. G. Brim (Eds.), *Life span development and behavior* (Vol. 2), pp. 117–159. New York: Academic Press.

Elder, G. H. (1981). History and the life course. In D. Bertaux (Ed.), *Biography and society*, pp. 77–115. Beverly Hills: Sage.

Elder, G. H. (Ed.). (1985). *Life course dynamics*. Ithaca: Cornell University Press.

Engelbert, A. (1986). Kinderalltag-familiale und ökologische Bedingungen. In K. Hurrelmann (Ed.), *Lebenslage, Lebensalter, Lebenszeit*. Weinheim: Beltz.

Epstein, J. L. (1987). Toward an integrated theory of family and school connections. In K. Hurrelmann, F. X. Kaufmann, & F. Lösel (Eds.), *Social intervention: Potential and constraints*, pp. 121–136. New York: De Gruyter.

Erikson, E. H. (1959). Identity and the life cycle. *Psychological Issues, 1*, 18–164.

Featherman, D. L., & Lerner, R. M. (1985). Ontogenesis and sociogenesis: Problematics for theory and research about development and socialization across the life span. *American Sociological Review, 50*, 659–676.

Fischer, C. S. (1982). To dwell among friends: Personal networks in town and city. Chicago: University of Chicago Press.

Flavell, J. H., & Ross, L. (Eds.). (1981). *Social cognitive development*. Cambridge: Cambridge University Press.

Frankenburg, W. K., Emde, R. N., & Sullivan, J. W. (Eds.). (1985). *Early identification of children at risk*. New York: Plenum.

150

References

Freud, S. (1923). *The ego and the id*. London: Hogarth.

Freud, S. (1949). *Outline of psychoanalysis*. New York: Norton.

Fthenakis, W. E. (1985). *Väter* (Vols. 1–2). Munich: Urban & Schwarzenberg.

Garbarino, J. (1982). *Children and families in the social environment*. New York: Aldine de Gruyter.

Garbarino, J., Schellenbach, C. J., & Sebes, J. M. (1986). *Troubled youth, troubled families*. New York: Aldine de Gruyter.

Gecas, V. (1979). The influence of social class on socialization. In W. R. Burr, R. Hill, F. J. Nye, J. C. Reiss (Eds.), *Contemporary theories about the family*, pp. 365–404. New York: Free Press.

Gecas, V. (1981). Contexts of socialization. In M. Rosenberg & R. Turner (Eds.), *Social psychology: Psychosocial perspectives*, pp. 165–199. New York: Basic Books.

Geulen, D. (1977). *Das vergesellschaftete Subjekt*. Frankfurt: Suhrkamp.

Geulen, D., & Hurrelmann, K. (1982). Toward a programme for a comprehensive theory of socialization. *Education, 26*, 39–60.

Gilligan, C. (1982). *In a different voice: Psychological theory and women's development*. Cambridge, Mass.: Harvard University Press.

Goffman, E. (1961). *Asylums: Essays on the social situation of mental patients and other inmates*. New York: Doubleday.

Goffman, E. (1963). *Stigma: Notes on the management of spoiled identity*. Englewood Cliffs: Prentice-Hall.

Goffman, E. (1972). *Encounters: Two studies in the sociology of interaction*. Harmondsworth: Penguin Books.

Goslin, D. (Ed.). (1969). *Handbook of socialization theory and research*. Chicago: Rand McNally.

Gottlieb, B. H. (1983). *Social support strategies*. Beverly Hills: Sage.

Gove, W. R. (1985). The effect of age and gender on deviant behavior: A biopsychological perspective. In A. S. Rossi (Ed.), *Gender and the life course*, pp. 115–144. New York: Aldine de Gruyter.

Grasso, J., & Shea, J. R. (1979). *Vocational education and training: Impact on youth*. Berkeley: Carnegie Council on Policy Studies in Higher Education.

Gurevitch, M., Bennett, T., Curran, J., & Woolacott, J. (Eds.). (1982). *Culture, society and the media*. London: Methuen.

Haan, N. (1981). Adolescents and young adults as producers of their development. In R. M. Lerner & N. A. Busch-Rossnagel (Eds.), *Individuals as producers of their development: A life span perspective*, pp. 155–182. New York: Academic Press.

Habermas, J. (1970). Toward a theory of communicative competence. *Inquiry, 13*, 360–375.

151

References

Habermas, J. (1976). *Zur Rekonstruktion des historischen Materialismus.* Frankfurt: Suhrkamp.

Habermas, J. (1984). *The theory of communicative action:* Vol. 1. *Reason and the rationalization of society.* Boston: Beacon Press.

Haferkamp, H. (1984). *Complexity and behavior structure.* Paper presented at conference of the German Sociological Association on relating micro- and macrolevels in sociological theory, Rauischholzhausen, West Germany, June 1984.

Hagemann-White, C. (1984). *Sozialisation: Weiblich–männlich?* Opladen: Leske & Budrich.

Hamburg, B. A., & Hamburg, D. A. (1975). Stressful transitions of adolescence: Endocrine and psychosocial aspects. In L. Levi (Ed.), *Society, stress, and disease* (Vol. 2), pp. 93–106. Oxford: Oxford University Press.

Hamilton, S. F. (1984). The secondary school in the ecology of adolescent development. In E. W. Gordon (Ed.), *Review of research in education,* pp. 227–258. New York: American Educational Research Association.

Hartup, W. H. (1984). Peer relations and the growth of social competence. In J. M. Joffe, G. W. Albee, & L. D. Kelly (Eds.), *Readings in primary prevention of psychopathology.* pp. 371–387. Hanover, N.H.: University Press of New England.

Hausser, K. (1983). *Identitätsentwicklung.* New York: Harper & Row.

Havighurst, R. J. (1972). *Developmental tasks and education* (3rd ed.). New York: McKay.

Heinz, W. (1980). Berufliche Sozialisation. In K. Hurrelmann & D. Ulich (Eds.), *Handbuch der Sozialisationsforschung,* pp. 499–520. Weinheim: Beltz.

Herzog, W. (1984). *Modell und Theorie in der Psychologie.* Göttingen: Hogrefe.

Hess, R. D., & Handel, G. (1959). *Family worlds.* Chicago: University of Chicago Press.

Heyns, B. (1978). *Summer learning and the effects of schooling.* New York: Academic Press.

Hirschi, T. (1969). *Causes of delinquency.* San Francisco: JAI Press.

Hoffman, M. L. (1963). Personality, family structure and social class as antecedents of parental power assertion. *Child Development, 34,* 869–884.

House, J. S. (1981). Social structure and personality. In M. Rosenberg & R. H. Turner (Eds.), *Social psychology: Sociological perspectives,* pp. 525–561. New York: Basic Books.

Hurrelmann, K. (1975). *Erziehungssystem und Gesellschaft.* Reinbek: Rowohlt.

References

Hurrelmann, K. (1984). Societal and organizational factors of stress on students in school. *European Journal of Teacher Education, 7,* 181–190.

Hurrelmann, K. (1985). *Toward a comprehensive theory of socialization.* Paper presented at the International Sociological Association conference on micro- and macro-perspectives in the sociology of education, Tel Aviv, April 1985.

Hurrelmann, K. (Ed.). (1986). *Lebenslage, Lebensalter, Lebenszeit.* Weinheim: Beltz.

Hurrelmann, K. (1987a). The limits and potential of social intervention in adolescence. In K. Hurrelmann, F. X. Kaufmann, & F. Lösel (Eds.), *Social intervention: Potential and constraints,* New York: De Gruyter.

Hurrelmann, K. (1987b). The importance of school in the life course. *Journal of Adolescent Research, 2,* 111–126.

Hurrelmann, K., Engel, U., Holler, B., & Nordlohne, E. (1988). Status insecurity and psychosomatic disorders in adolescence. *Journal of Adolescence.*

Hurrelmann, K., Kaufmann, F. X., & Lösel, F. (Eds.). (1987). *Social intervention: Potential and constraints.* New York: De Gruyter.

Hurrelmann, K., & Ulich, D. (Eds.). (1982). *Handbuch der Sozialisationsforschung* (2nd ed.) Weinheim: Beltz.

Hurrelmann, K., Rosewitz, B., & Wolf, H. K. (1985). *Lebensphase Jugend.* Munich: Juventa.

Inkeles, A. (1968). Society, social structure and child socialization. In J. A. Clausen, *Socialization and society,* pp. 73–129. Boston: Little, Brown.

Jessor, R., & Jessor, S. L. (1977). *Problem behavior and psychological development.* New York: Academic Press.

Jick, T. D. (1979). Mixing qualitative and quantitative methods: Triangulation in action. *Administrative Science Quarterly, 24,* 602–611.

Joas, H. (1980). *Praktische Intersubjektivität: Die Entwicklung des Werkes von G. H. Mead.* Frankfurt: Suhrkamp.

Johnson, J. H. (1986). *Life events as stressors in childhood and adolescence.* Beverly Hills: Sage.

Kaufmann, F. X. (1987). Prevention and intervention in the analytical perspective of guidance. In K. Hurrelmann, F. X. Kaufmann, & F. Lösel (Eds.), *Social intervention: Potential and constraints,* pp. 3–20. New York: De Gruyter.

Kerckhoff, A. C. (1972). *Socialization and social class.* Englewood Cliffs: Prentice-Hall.

Kerckhoff, A. C., & Corwin, R. G. (Eds.). (1981). *Research in sociology of education and socialization.* Vol. 2. *Research on educational organizations.* San Francisco: JAI Press.

References

Knorr-Cetina, K., & Cicourel, A. V. (Eds.) (1981). *Advances in social theory and methodology*. Boston: Henley.

Kohlberg, L. (1963). Stage and sequence: The cognitive-developmental approach to socialization. In D. A. Goslin (Ed.), *Handbook of socialization theory and research*, pp. 347–480. Chicago: Rand McNally.

Kohli, M. (1980). Lebenslauftheoretische Ansätze in der Sozialisationsforschung. In K. Hurrelmann & D. Ulich (Eds.), *Handbuch der Sozialisationsforschung*, pp. 299–320. Weinheim: Beltz.

Kohli, M. (1986). Social organization and subjective construction of the life course. In A. B. Sorensen, F. E. Weinert, & L. R. Sherrod (Eds.), *Human development and the life course*, pp. 271–292. Hillsdale, N.J.: Erlbaum.

Kohn, M. L. (1969). *Class and conformity: A study in values*. New York: Dorsey.

Kohn, M. L., & Schooler, C. (Eds.). (1983). *Work and personality*. Norwood, N.J.: Ablex.

Krappman, L. (1969).*Soziologische Dimensionen der Identität*. Stuttgart: Klett.

Lamb, M. E. (Ed.). (1976). *The role of the father in child development*. New York: Wiley.

Laosa, L. M., & Sigel, I. E. (Eds.). (1982). *Families as learning environments for children*. New York: Plenum.

Lazarsfeld, P. F., & Rosenberg, M. (Eds.) (1955). *The language of social research*. Glencoe, Ill.: Free Press.

Lazarus, R. S., & Launier, R. (1978). Stress-related transaction between person and environment. In L. Pervin & M. Lewis (Eds.), *Perspectives in interactional psychology*, pp. 287–327. New York: Plenum.

Leontjev, A. N. (1964). *Problems of mental development*. New York: Pergamon Press.

Lerner, R. M. (1975). *Concepts and theories of human development*. Reading, Mass.: Addison-Wesley.

Lerner, R. M., & Busch-Rossnagel, N. A. (1981). Individuals as producers of their development. In R. M. Lerner & N. A. Busch-Rossnagel (Eds.), *Individuals as producers of their development: A life span perspective*, pp. 1–36. New York: Academic Press.

Lerner, R. M., & Spanier, G. (1980). *Adolescent development: A life span perspective*. New York: McGraw-Hill.

Looft, W. R. (1973). Socialization and personality through the life span. In P. B. Baltes & K. W. Schaie (Eds.), *Life span developmental psychology*, pp. 25–52. New York: Academic Press.

Lorenzer, A. (1972). *Zur Begründung einer materialistischen Sozialisationstheorie*. Frankfurt: Suhrkamp.

References

Luhmann, N. (1982). *The differentiation of society.* New York: Columbia University Press.

Luhmann, N. (1984). *Soziale Systeme.* Frankfurt: Suhrkamp.

Maccoby, E. E., & Martin, J. A. (1984): Socialization in the context of the family: Parent–child interaction. In E. M. Hetherington (Ed.), *Handbook of child psychology* (Vol. 4), pp. 1–102. New York: Wiley.

Magnusson, D., & Allen, V. L. (Eds.). (1983). *Human development: An interactional perspective.* New York: Academic Press.

Marx, Karl. (1966). Oekonomisch-philosophische Manuskripte von 1844. In Karl Marx, *Texte zu Methode und Praxis* (Vol. 2), pp. 7–133. Reinbek: Rowohlt.

Mattejat, F. (1985). *Familie und psychische Störungen.* Stuttgart: Enke.

Mayer, K. U., & Müller, W. (1986). The state and the structure of the life course. In A. B. Sorensen, F. E. Weinert, & L. R. Sherrod (Eds.), *Human development and the life course,* pp. 217–245. Hillsdale, N.J.: Erlbaum.

Mead, G. H. (1934). *Mind, self and society.* Chicago: University of Chicago Press.

Meyer, J. W. (1986). The self and the life course: Institutionalization and its effects. In A. B. Sorensen, F. E. Weinert, & L. R. Sherrod (Eds.), *Human development and the life course,* pp. 217–245. Hillsdale, N.J.: Erlbaum.

Meyer, J. W., & Rowan, B. (1983). The structure of educational organizations. In J. W. Meyer & W. R. Scott (Eds.), *Organizational environments: Ritual and rationality,* pp. 71–98. London: Sage.

Moriarty, A. E., & Toussieng, M. D. (1976). *Adolescent coping.* New York: Grune & Stratton.

Mortimer, J. L., Lawrence, J., & Kumka, D. (1986). *Work, family and personality: Transition to adulthood.* Norwood, N.J.: Ablex.

Nesselroade, J. R., & Baltes, P. B. (Eds.). (1979) *Longitudinal research in the study of behavior and development.* New York: Academic Press.

Nesselroade, J. R., & Van Eye, A. (Eds.). (1985). *Individual development and social change.* New York: Academic Press.

Neugarten, B. L., & Hagestad, G. O. (1985). Age and the life course. In R. H. Binstock & E. Shanas (Eds.), *Handbook of aging and the social sciences,* pp. 35–55. New York: Van Nostrand Reinhold.

Newman, B. M., & Newman, P. R. (1975). *Development through life.* Homewood, Ill.: Dorsey.

Oerter, R., & Montada, L. (Eds.). (1987). *Entwicklungpsychologie.* Munich: Urban & Schwarzenberg.

Ottomeyer, K. (1980). Gesellschaftstheorien in der Sozialisationsforschung. In K. Hurrelmann & D. Ulich (Eds.), *Handbuch der Sozialisationsforschung,* pp. 161–196. Weinheim: Beltz.

References

Overtone, W. F., & Reese, H. W. (1973). Models of development: Methodological implications. In J. R. Nesselroade & H. W. Reese (Eds.), *Life span developmental psychology: Methodological issues*. New York: Academic Press.

Parsons, T. (1964). *Social structure and personality*. New York: Free Press.

Parsons, T., & Bales, R. F. (1955). *Family, socialization and interaction process*. Glencoe, Ill.: Free Press.

Pearlin, L. (1983). Role strain and personal stress. In H. B. Kaplan (Ed.), *Psychosocial stress: Trends in theory and research*, pp. 6–32. New York: Academic Press.

Pearlin, L. (1987). The stress process and strategies of intervention. In K. Hurrelmann, F. X. Kaufmann, & F. Lösel, *Social intervention: Potential and constraints*, pp. 53–72. New York: De Gruyter.

Persell, C. H. (1977). *Education and inequality*. New York: Free Press.

Persell, C. H. (1984). *Understanding society*. New York: Harper & Row.

Petersen, A. C., & Ebata, A. (1987). Developmental transitions and adolescent problem behavior, In K. Hurrelmann, F. X. Kaufmann, & F. Lösel (Eds.), *Social intervention: Potential and constraints*, pp. 167–184. New York: De Gruyter.

Petri, H. (1979). *Soziale Schicht und psychische Erkrankung im Kindes- und Jugendalter*. Göttingen: Vandenhoek & Ruprecht.

Piaget, J. (1950). *The psychology of intelligence*. London: Routledge & Kegan Paul.

Piaget, J. (1970). Piaget's theory. In P. H. Mussen (Ed.), *Carmichael's manual of child psychology* (Vol. 1). New York: Wiley.

Plake, K. (1981). *Die Sozialisationsorganisationen*. Opladen: Westdeutscher Verlag.

Riegel, K. (1975). Towards a dialectical theory of development. In *Human Development, 18*, 50–64.

Riley, M. W. (1985). Age strata in social systems. In R. H. Binstock & E. Shanas (Eds.), *Handbook on aging and the social sciences*, pp. 189–217. New York: Van Nostrand Reinhold.

Rosenberg, M. (1981). The self-concept: Social product and social force. In M. Rosenberg & R. H. Turner (Eds.), *Social psychology: Sociological perspectives*, pp. 593–624. New York: Basic Books.

Rosenberg, M., & Gara, M. A. (1985). The multiplicity of personal identity. In P. Shaver (Ed.), *Self, situations, and social behavior*. Beverly Hills: Sage.

Rosenmayr, L. (Ed.). (1978). *Die menschlichen Lebensalter: Kontinuität und Krisen*. Munich; Piper.

Rossi, A. (Ed.). (1985). *Gender and the life course*. New York: Aldine de Gruyter.

References

Runyan, W. M. (1978). The life course as a theoretical orientation: Sequences of person–situation interaction. *Journal of Personality, 46,* 569–593.

Rutter, M. (1980). *Changing youth in a changing society.* Cambridge Mass.: Harvard University Press.

Rutter, M., Maugham, B., Mortimore, P., Ouston, J., & Smith, A. (1979). *Fifteen thousand hours: Secondary schools and their effects on children.* London: Open Books.

Schneewind, K. A., Beckmann, H., & Engfer, A. (1983). *Eltern und Kinder: Umwelteinflüsse auf das familiäre Verhalten.* Stuttgart: Kohlhammer.

Schorb, B., Mohn, E., & Theunert, H. (1980). Sozialisation durch Massenmedien. In K. Hurrelmann & D. Ulich (Eds.), *Handbuch der Sozialisationsforschung,* pp. 306–330. Weinheim: Beltz.

Seidman, E. (Ed.). (1983). *Handbook of social intervention.* London: Sage.

Seiler, T. B. (1980). Entwicklungstheorien in der Sozialisationsforschung. In K. Hurrelmann & D. Ulich (Eds.), *Handbuch der Sozialisationsforschung,* pp. 101–122. Weinheim: Beltz.

Sève, L. (1972). *Marxisme et la theorie de la personalite.* Paris: Editions Sociales.

Sewell, W. H., & Hauser, R. M. (1975). *Education, occupation and earnings,* New York: Academic Press.

Sieber, S. D. (1973). The integration of fieldwork and survey methods. *American Journal of Sociology, 78,* 1335–1359.

Sigel, I. E., & Laosa, L. M. (Eds.). (1983). *Changing families.* New York: Plenum.

Silbereisen, R. K., & Eyferth, K. (1986). Development as action in context. In R. K. Silbereisen, K. Eyferth, & G. Rudinger (Eds.), *Development as action in context,* pp. 3–16. Berlin: Springer.

Silbereisen, R. K., Noack, P., & Reitzle, M. (1987). Developmental perspectives on problem behavior and prevention in adolescence. In K. Hurrelmann, F. X. Kaufmann, & F. Lösel (Eds.), *Social intervention: Potential and contraints,* pp. 205–218. New York: De Gruyter.

Skinner, B. F. (1938). *The behavior of organisms.* New York: Appleton.

Sorensen, A. B., Weinert, F. E., & Sherrod, L. R. (Eds.). (1986). *Human development and the life course.* Hillsdale, N.J.: Erlbaum.

Steinkamp, G. (1980). Klassen- und schichtspezifische Ansätze in der Sozialisationsforschung. In K. Hurrelmann & D. Ulich (Eds.), *Handbuch der Sozialisationsforschung,* pp. 253–284. Weinheim: Beltz.

Swanson, G. E. (1974). Family structure and the reflective intelligence of children. *Sociometry, 37,* 459–490.

References

Ulich, D. (1980). Lern- und Verhaltenstheorien in der Sozialisationsforschung. In K. Hurrelmann & D. Ulich (Eds.), *Handbuch der Sozialisationsforschung*, pp. 71–100. Weinheim: Beltz.

Vondra, J. I. (1986). Socioeconomic stress and family functioning in adolescence. In J. Garbarino, C. J. Schellenbach, & J. M. Sebes (Eds.), *Troubled youth, troubled families*, pp. 191–233. New York: Aldine de Gruyter.

Wagner, D. G. (1984). *The growth of sociological theories.* London: Sage.

Weinstein, E. A. (1969). The development of interpersonal competence. In D. Goslin (Ed.), *Handbook of socialization theory and research*, pp. 753–775. Chicago: Rand McNally.

Wentworth, W. M. (1980). *Context and understanding: An inquiry into socialization theory.* New York: Elsevier.

Woods, P., & Hammersley, M. (Eds.). (1977). *School experience.* New York: St. Martin's Press.

Wrong, D. (1961). The oversocialized conception of man in modern sociology. *American Sociological Review, 26,* 183–193.

Youniss, J. (1980). *Parents and peers in social development.* Chicago: Chicago University Press.

NAME INDEX

Name index

Erikson, E. H., 14, 114, 116
Eye, A. van, 60, 134
Eyferth, K., 21, 49, 128

Featherman, D. L., 6, 22, 43
Fischer, C. S., 126
Flavell, J. H., 48, 107
Frankenburg, W. K., 123
Freud, S., 12–14, 102
Fthenakis, W. E., 88

Gara, M. A., 114
Garbarino, J., 88, 92, 129, 130
Gecas, V., 47, 70, 80, 83
Geulen, D., 5, 39, 41, 44, 72, 73
Gilligan, C., 131
Goffman, E., 66, 110, 111, 114
Goslin, D., 3
Gottlieb, B. H., 52, 125, 126, 137
Gove, W. R., 131, 132
Grasso, J., 98
Grunebaum, H., 134
Gugler, B., 50
Gurevitch, M., 67

Haan, N., 49, 61, 100, 125
Habermas, J., 18, 32–36, 41, 50, 64, 115, 116
Haferkamp, H., 31, 41
Hagemann-White, C., 133
Hagestad, G. O., 100
Hamburg, B. A., 44
Hamburg, D. A., 44
Hamilton, S. F., 144
Hammersley, M., 95
Handel, G., 88
Hartup, W. P., 144
Hauser, R. M., 95
Hausser, K., 111
Havighurst, R. J., 49, 108
Heinz, W., 98, 99
Herzog, W., 17
Hess, R. D., 88
Heyns, B., 70
Hirschi, T., 121
Hoffman, M. L., 74
Holler, B., 97, 132
Honzik, M. P., 61, 100

House, J. S., 47
Hurrelmann, K., 3, 6, 39, 44, 48, 52, 55, 61, 68, 70–73, 77, 90, 95–100, 109, 117, 121, 132–5

Indermühle, K., 50
Inkeles, A., 46

Jessor, R., 122, 125
Jessor, S. L., 122, 125
Jick, T. D., 59
Joas, H., 32
Johnson, J. H., 143
Johnston, J., 123

Kagan, F., 48, 107, 118
Kalbermatten, U., 50
Kaufmann, F. X., 52, 133, 134
Kerckhoff, A. C., 3, 69, 74
Knorr-Cetina, K., 41
Kohlberg, L., 18
Kohli, M., 3, 48, 101, 102, 118
Kohn, M. L., 65, 74, 79–81, 87, 99
Krappmann, L., 114
Kumka, D., 89

Lamb, M. E., 88
Laosa, L. M., 85, 129
Launier, R., 124, 125
Lawrence, F., 89
Lazarsfeld, P. F., 53
Lazarus, R. S., 124, 125
Leontjev, A. N., 33
Lerner, R. M., 3, 6, 22, 43, 48, 49
Levin, H. M., 68, 69
Lipsitt, L., 23
Looft, W. R., 5
Lorenzer, A., 14
Lösel, F., 52, 134
Luckmann, T., 46
Luhmann, N., 27–28, 64

Maccoby, E. E., 10, 56–57
Magnusson, D., 22
Marlin, M. M., 91
Martin, J. A., 10, 56–57
Marx, K., 32–33
Mattejat, F., 122, 131

160

Name index

Maugham, B., 71
Mayer, K. U., 100
Mead, G. H., 28–32, 33, 41, 112–113, 114
Meyer, J. W., 68, 119
Michelson, L., 134, 137
Mohn, E., 67
Montada, L., 4
Moriarty, A. E., 125
Mortimer, J. L., 89
Mortimore, P., 71
Müller, W., 100
Mussen, P. H., 61, 100

Nesselroade, J. R., 60
Neugarten, B. L., 100
Newman, B. M., 48, 109
Newman, P. R., 48, 109
Noack, P., 138
Nordlohne, E., 97, 132

Oerter, R., 4
O'Malley, P., 123
Ottomeyer, K., 32
Ouston, J., 71
Overtone, W. F., 6

Palmonari, A., 18, 89, 107
Parsons, T., 24–27, 102
Passeron, J., 68
Pearlin, L., 52, 124
Persell, C. H., 76, 78, 95
Petersen, A. C., 122
Petri, H., 122
Piaget, J., 15–18
Plake, K., 66

Reese, H. W., 6, 23
Reitzle, M., 138
Riegel, K., 22
Riley, M. W., 100
Rosenberg, M., 53, 111, 112, 113, 128
Rosenmayr, L., 100
Rosewitz, B., 48, 71, 72, 90, 109, 117
Ross, L., 48, 107
Rossi, A., 133
Rowan, B., 68

Runyan, W. M., 100
Rutter, M., 71, 121, 122, 132

Schellenbach, C. J., 92, 129
Schneewind, K. A., 85, 129
Schooler, C., 65, 79, 87, 99
Schorb, B., 67
Sebes, F. M., 92, 129
Seidman, E., 134
Seiler, T. B., 17
Sève, L., 33
Sewell, W. H., 95
Shea, J. R., 98
Sherrod, L. R., 100
Sieber, S. D., 59
Sigel, I. E., 85, 129
Silbereisen, R. K., 21, 49, 128, 138
Simmons, R. G., 100
Skinner, B. F., 11
Smith, A., 71
Sommerkorn, I. N., 80
Sorenson, A. B., 100
Spanier, G., 48
Steinkamp, G., 87
Sullivan, J. W., 123
Swanson, G. E., 82

Taylor, S. J., 53
Theunert, H., 67
Toussieng, M. D., 125

Ulich, D., 3, 11, 61

Vondra, J. I., 129

Wagner, D. G., 5
Weinert, F. E., 100
Weinstein, E. A., 112
Wentworth, W. M., 1, 3, 26, 40, 41, 63
Wheeler, S., 65
Wolf, H. K., 48, 71, 72, 90, 109, 117
Woods, P., 95
Woolacott, J., 67
Wrong, D., 27

Youniss, J., 90, 143

161

SUBJECT INDEX